SHAKYAMUNI
BUDDHA

SHAKYAMUNI BUDDHA
A Narrative Biography

by Nikkyō Niwano

Tokyo • KŌSEI PUBLISHING CO.

Reproduced on the front cover is a portion of a modern copy of the hanging scroll *The Nirvana of the Buddha,* painted in 1086. The copy, executed by Ryūsen Miyahara, is owned by Risshō Kōsei-kai and is used by permission. The original scroll, owned by the temple Kongōbu-ji in Wakayama Prefecture, has been designated a National Treasure by the Japanese government. The device used on the title page and chapter-opening pages is an ancient Buddhist iconographic symbol: a trident representing the Three Treasures that rests on a stylized lotus, which may represent both the Lotus Sutra and the Wheel of the Law.

This book was originally published in Japanese as part 2 of *Bukkyō no Inochi Hokekyō.* Translation by Kojirō Miyasaka adapted by Rebecca M. Davis.

Cover design and layout of photographs by Nobu Miyazaki. Editing, book design, and typography by Rebecca M. Davis. The text of this book is set in monotype Plantin with handset De Vinne Condensed for display.

Revised English edition, 1980
Fourth printing, 1985

Contents

Preface

FOR SOME TIME NOW I have wanted to see a plain, readable biography of Shakyamuni, the historical Buddha, published in English. Although there is a growing number of books on his teachings available in English, it occurred to me that there is no introductory biography for people who might be curious about the life of this great religious leader.

I envisioned a biography that simply related the life of the founder of Buddhism and the lives of those closest to him without spending a great deal of time explaining or interpreting his profound teachings or the history and sociology of ancient India. In *The Lotus Sutra: Life and Soul of Buddhism,* a book I wrote some years ago about the Lotus Sutra, one of the most important scriptures of Mahayana Buddhism, I included basically the sort of biography I speak of. With encouragement from readers of that book I have undertaken the publication of this completely revised version of that biography.

The account of the life of the Buddha offered here is

taken from classical Buddhist sources—principally the Agama sutras, among the oldest of Buddhist scriptures, and the *Buddhacharita,* a second-century A.D. biography of the Buddha—although I have sometimes included incidents recorded in other sources. I have also quoted occasionally from the Lotus Sutra, and all those quotations are taken from *The Threefold Lotus Sutra,* translated by Bunno Kato et al., which was jointly published in 1975 by the Kosei Publishing Co. and John Weatherhill, Inc., of New York and Tokyo.

Because the Buddhist documents that I have used as sources were originally recorded in Sanskrit, all the personal and place names and terms in this book are transliterated from the Sanskrit, regardless of whether the Pali form of a word (Gotama, for instance) may be better known to some readers than the Sanskrit (Gautama). And because my intention in preparing this book has been to make the Buddha's life story readily comprehensible to modern readers, I have used a simplified Sanskrit transliteration throughout; for example, "Śākyamuni" is always rendered as "Shakyamuni." However, the orthodox transliterations of these words, with proper diacritical marks, are included in the glossary.

Since I have purposely refrained from discussing the Buddha's teachings and the doctrines of Buddhism in this book, perhaps I should offer a word to readers interested in further information. One of Japan's foremost scholars of Buddhism, Professor Kogen Mizuno of Komazawa University, has written two fine introductory works on Buddhism, *The Beginnings of Buddhism* and *Primitive Buddhism,* both published in English by the Kosei Publishing Co.; and my own *Buddhism for Today: A New Interpretation of the Threefold Lotus Sutra,* published jointly by the Kosei Publishing

Co. and John Weatherhill, Inc., may also be of interest.

It is my sincere hope that *Shakyamuni Buddha: A Narrative Biography* will help many people understand the life of the historical Buddha, and if even one reader of this book is stimulated to further reading I shall feel fully rewarded.

SHAKYAMUNI
BUDDHA

1 · From Prince
to Peerless Sage

THE BIRTH The historical Buddha, the founder of Buddhism, was born in northeastern India about twenty-five hundred years ago. The firstborn son of King Shuddhodana, he was named Siddhartha, literally, "he who has accomplished his aim." Shuddhodana was the ruler of the Shakya state—which, as was the custom in India at that time, was known by the name of the ruling tribe, rather than by the name of the land it occupied.

The country of the Shakyas was not an absolute monarchy. It was organized as an aristocratic council-system republic, ruled by the mutual consent of the members of the tribe and its governing class. Shuddhodana, who was chief among the aristocratic class of the tribe, was designated the *rajan,* or ruler. The state of the Shakyas was a small country extending from the northern border of India into what is now southern Nepal. The remains of its capital city, Kapilavastu, and the palace in which the Buddha grew up still survive to remind us of the days when the land of the Shakyas was a vital minor state in northern India.

Today it is widely believed that the Shakya tribe was descended not from the Aryan invaders of what is present-day India but from peoples of Mongolian origin. The tribe, which is said to have been generally peaceful and hard working, engaged primarily in agriculture.

The family name of the founder of Buddhism was Gautama. Though called Siddhartha from birth, after he attained enlightenment and achieved buddhahood he was called Shakyamuni, literally, the "Sage [*muni*] of the Shakyas." He was also called *Bhagavat*, or World-honored One, when people addressed him directly. Today we refer to the historical Buddha as Lord Shakyamuni or simply Shakyamuni; to refer to him as Shakya alone is meaningless, since it is only the name of the tribe into which he was born. Shakyamuni referred to himself as the Tathagata, meaning "one who has reached the truth and come to declare it"; this is why we often use the appellation Tathagata Shakyamuni when referring to Shakyamuni specifically as a buddha.

We also refer to Shakyamuni as simply the Buddha. Because "buddha" has acquired numerous interpretations, I should like to discuss it briefly here in the context of Mahayana Buddhism.

The word *buddha* comes to us from Sanskrit, the classical liturgical and literary language of ancient India, and means "one who is enlightened" or "enlightened one." Shakyamuni taught that there had been many buddhas, or "enlightened ones," in the past; but from our point of view, he is the sole historical Buddha. Frequently, the word buddha means not only a living being who has realized the truth, but the great eternal life-force that is the source of all existences in this universe. This interpretation, which is basic to Mahayana Buddhism, is founded on the words of Shakyamuni as recorded in chapter 16 of the Lotus Sutra, "Revelation of the [Eternal] Life of the Tathagata," in which he explains that the Buddha is eternal, having existed from the infinite past and appearing in many forms throughout the ages to guide and succor beings, and that the Eternal Buddha is the source of existence, the source of the life-force that permeates all beings.

Shuddhodana and his people had long awaited the birth of an heir to the king. As was the custom in those days, when the time for her confinement drew near Maya, Shuddhodana's queen—a princess of the royal house of Koliya—wished to return to her family home to give birth. Having journeyed as far as Lumbini Garden, roughly thirty kilometers from Kapilavastu, Maya paused to rest for a while. Another account says that she went to Lumbini Garden for her health after having gone to the home of her father, in Devadaha, the capital of Koliya.

Lumbini Garden is said to have been a picturesque park with many-colored flowers in bloom, pure streams in a beautiful forest, and scattered ponds, although no traces of a beautiful forest or ponds now remain. While Queen Maya was strolling in the garden, accompanied by her many attendants, she suddenly felt labor pains. According to legend, when the queen reached out to pluck flowering branch from an *ashoka* tree, a perfect child was born and Brahma and Indra, two of the chief Hindu deities, descended from heaven and reverently took the infant in their arms. It is also said that upon his birth the infant took seven steps in each of the cardinal directions and, with his right hand raised toward heaven and his left extended toward the earth (in the mudra of bestowing fearlessness and charity), declared, "I alone am honored, in heaven and on earth."

Chronicles of the lives of great men of the distant past often contain highly symbolic or miraculous incidents like this. Their frequent occurrence in early biographies of the historical Buddha led many Western scholars to believe that Shakyamuni was only a fiction invented by people of later ages. Moreover, magnified stories, like that of the Buddha's birth, often make people feel that Buddhism is a religion far removed from real life. Such a judgment arises from confusing "fact" with "truth." The people of ancient India emphasized the truth of something (the significance of the Buddha's birth, for instance) by not restricting themselves to absolute factual accuracy.

For example, one of the oldest works of Buddhist art in India, a relief from an ancient stupa at Bharhut, depicts the founding of the Jetavana Monastery, which was built by Sudatta, a rich merchant in Shravasti, the capital of Kaushala, the greatest of the Indian kingdoms of that time. This relief is based on the following story, which is no less true even if some of its facts are not absolutely correct. Sudatta, who was a devout follower of the Buddha, selected some land south of Shravasti on which to build a monastery for Shakyamuni. Because the grove he chose belonged to the Kaushala prince Jeta, Sudatta asked the prince to name a price. In jest Prince Jeta replied, "If you were to cover all the ground with gold, I would sell it to you." Taking the prince seriously, Sudatta set about laying gold over the land. Astonished by Sudatta's enthusiasm and deep devotion to Shakyamuni, the prince donated the gold to pay for constructing buildings for the monastery.

In the center of the relief, Sudatta stands holding a jar in his hands. It is said that the jar was used for the purificatory water that Indian custom required for the ground-breaking ceremony. Sudatta with the jar represents the ground-breaking ceremony, while at the right is depicted the scene of the gold being laid over the land. At the left, Prince Jeta is shown in his palace with his followers, who hold their hands near their faces in the mudra of reverence or adoration, with the palms joined. Completed structures of the Jetavana Monastery appear above and below the scene with the prince. (One explanation of the scene in the palace says that the mudra of Prince Jeta's followers depicts worship of the bo, or pipal, tree, one of the symbols used to represent Shakyamuni in ancient Buddhist art, since it was beneath a bo tree that he attained enlightenment.)

An integrated portrayal that brings together deities and people and events of different times and places is common in the arts of ancient India. This kind of representation is frequently encountered in accounts of the Buddha's life. We have already considered the legend concerning the birth of the Buddha that says he immediately took seven steps in each of the cardinal directions and announced, "I alone am honored, in heaven and on earth." This legend merges the fact of the Buddha's birth with the fact that in his later years he became a great and honored sage who proclaimed his teachings in all directions.

Symbolic expressions of the sort just mentioned are found throughout the sutras. They are not meant to be interpreted literally, any more than we would attach a literal interpretation to the words of someone who said, "I was convulsed with laughter." But even if such expressions are not factually true, they do communicate vividly and effectively genuine belief, admiration, or spiritual experiences.

A person who accepts fact alone cannot appreciate literature or art; suspension of disbelief enables us to comprehend intangible ideas expressed in tangible form. Thus if in Buddhist texts we encounter things that seem impossible, we should consider the truth, or meaning, lying behind the "facts" without being misled by the form of expression.

REALIZING THE SUFFERING OF LIFE   Seven days after Prince Siddhartha's birth, his mother died suddenly. Her younger sister, Mahaprajapati, became his foster mother, and under her care he grew up secure, for she showed him no less love than his real mother had. It is traditionally said that he was a sensitive and contemplative boy, traits that could have been due in part to the early death of his mother.

One spring day the local farmers held a plowing ceremony outside the palace as part of an annual agricultural festival. Together with his father and many retainers, Prince Siddhartha attended this ceremony and for the first time watched the farmers at their arduous work. He was deeply affected by the pained expressions of the farmers who, bathed in perspiration, plowed the hard earth beneath the glaring sun. He was yet more troubled when he noticed birds descend and snatch small worms and insects that had been exposed by the farmers' plows. The worms and insects vainly tried to escape death.

Unable to bear watching such a painful scene, the prince left the festival and went to sit in the shade in a nearby forest, where he fell into deep thought.—One living creature eats another living creature. One creature kills another so that it may live. How cruel this is! Yet it is actually done.—Though he was still but a youth, he felt acutely that all life is suffering.

When the king and his retainers realized the prince had disappeared, they went in search of him and found him under a tree, lost in meditation. It is said that King Shuddhodana involuntarily bowed his head at the inspiring figure of his son.

Realizing early that his son had the potential to become a man of religion, the king was both pleased and worried. Following the custom of the time, Shuddhodana had summoned some eminent seers soon after Siddhartha's birth and had had the child's destiny predicted. The seers declared to the king unanimously, "This prince has the strong facial features that indicate he will be a great man in the future. If when grown he succeeds to the throne, he will become a great king and rule all the world, not by armed might but by virtue. But if he gives up his throne to enter the religious life, he will become a buddha and save all the people of the world from their sufferings."

This prediction was confirmed by the famous hermit-seer Asita, who lived far away in the mountains. In India today, there are many yogis with paranormal abilities, but there were many more such people in ancient India, and Asita was one of them. Through his abilities, Asita was aware that the future Buddha had been born in Kapilavastu, and so with his disciple he left the distant mountains and made his way to the palace. Taking the prince in his arms, Asita burst into tears and cried, "A great man has appeared in the world at last!"

Alarmed by Asita's tears, the king asked the seer, "Is there cause for worry about my son?" Asita replied, "I have but a few years left. I can neither see the day when

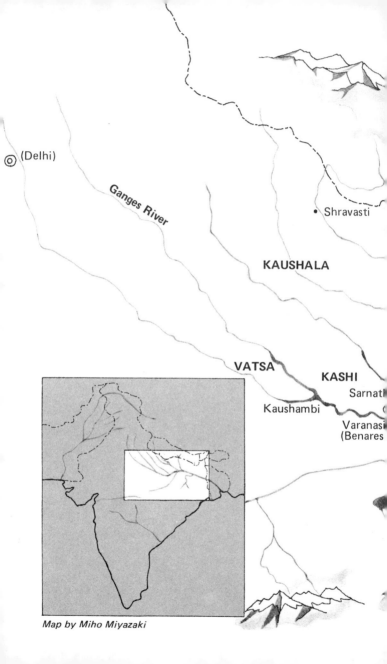

Map by Miho Miyazaki

Shakyamuni's India

umbini
apilavastu(?)
prahwa)

KOLIYAS

HAKYAS

Kushinagara
MALLA

VRIJIS

•Vaishali

Pataliputra (Patna)

Rajagriha (Rajgir)
•Gaya

(Bodh Gaya)

MAGADHA

Champa

ANGA

Ganges River

KAUSHALA——*Ancient kingdoms*
Lumbini————*Ancient place names*
(Rajgir)————*Modern place names*

(Calcutta)◉

this prince will become a buddha nor listen to the true teaching preached by him. My heart is anguished by that thought."

At first pleased with Asita's prophecy that his son would become a great man, the king later became concerned over the possibility of Siddhartha's leaving the palace to renounce the world. In all possible ways Shuddhodana tried to make the prince enjoy life in the palace and to divert his attention from distressing thoughts. The king gave Siddhartha different palaces for summer, winter, spring, and autumn. Shuddhodana looked after his son so carefully that the prince, who was waited upon by many servants, wanted for nothing.

Thus the daily life of the prince was very happy. Like the sons of other aristocrats, the prince worked hard at his lessons in literature, the martial arts, and sports. It is said that he was especially good at sports, including archery, wrestling, running, and jumping. However, during this happy youth his religious disposition also began to develop and become increasingly evident, and finally he became determined to become a monk. One account of the life of the Buddha gives the following explanation of that decision.

One day the prince told his retainers to prepare for an outing to a park some distance away. Hearing of this, King Shuddhodana ordered the removal of all unclean and unsightly things along the road. He also had flowers scattered and incense placed all along the road so the route would seem an earthly paradise. He even gave orders that the aged, the ill, and the crippled should not appear by the roadside.

Despite all those precautions, when the prince left the eastern gate of the palace he beheld an old man tottering down the road. The man was little more than a skeleton, and his back was so bent he could barely stand erect even with the aid of a staff. He was short of breath and not a tooth was visible in his half-open, drooling mouth. The prince, unable to bear the distressing sight, asked one of his retainers, "Who is this person?"

Reluctantly the retainer replied, "He is an old man."

"An old man? What is that?"

"As more and more time passes after birth, a person becomes infirm, decrepit, and helpless. Such a person is neglected by those around him, and to increase his misery, he has only a few remaining years to live. That is the way with an old man."

"Is he alone in this affliction of old age that you have described to me?"

"No, at some time everyone becomes like that old man. There is no difference between nobles and people of humble birth. No one can escape the suffering of aging and old age."

The retainer's words set Siddhartha thinking. An excursion to the park no longer seemed pleasurable. The prince told his charioteer to return to the palace immediately.

For some time afterward Siddhartha had no opportunity to leave the palace again, but one day he left from the southern gate, to avoid the eastern gate, through which he had passed earlier. He saw lying by the roadside a sick person who moaned and then turned and fell in his own vomit.

The prince asked his retainer, "Who is this person?"

The retainer answered, "He is a sick person."

"What is a sick person?"

"That is a person who is out of sorts and is no longer master of himself. No living being can escape sickness at some time."

Deeply troubled, the prince again returned to the palace.

On the next occasion, as he left from the western gate, he noticed a large funeral procession.

The prince asked his retainer, "What is that?"

The retainer replied, "That is the procession for a person who has died."

"What is death?"

"It means that a person's spirit leaves his body, and he loses the awareness and vitality of his life. Death permanently prohibits him from seeing the people near to him, such as his parents, brothers, sisters, spouse, and children."

"Must a person die?"

"Yes, whoever was born into this world must someday die."

Those words affected Siddhartha deeply, and in sorrow he gave up his outing and returned to the palace.

On another day the prince again desired to leave the palace, and that time he left by the northern gate. Coming toward him he saw a monk with shaven head and face who seemed quite hale. The man, who was neatly dressed in a brown robe, carried a monk's staff, and his eyes were filled with compassion. Slowly he approached the prince.

The prince asked his retainer, "Who is this person?"

The retainer answered, "He is a monk, one who endeavors to practice virtue and to cease doing evil."

Alighting from his carriage, the prince stood before the monk, greeted him, and asked, "What kind of divine favor have you received in your religious life as a monk?"

The monk replied, "When I was still a layman, I soberly contemplated the four sufferings of birth, aging, sickness, and death, and I realized that all things in this world are always changing. By leading the life of a monk and striving to practice religious disciplines in a quiet place, I was able to transcend various sufferings. I now hope to give true peace and happiness to many people. I am one who will eternally set himself apart from the defilement of the world. I think this is the divine favor a monk can receive."

Listening to the monk's words, the prince said, "It is exactly as you say. The way of the monk is that which I have been seeking."

Suddenly the prince was elated. Cheerfully he continued to the park, where he amused himself the whole day; and in the evening, when he returned to the palace after bathing in a pond, he felt refreshed in mind and body.

At the time of this story, called the "Outings from the Four Gates," the prince is said to have been nearing thirty years of age and already married. We can then infer that this was not the first time he had seen an old person, a sick person, or a dead person; but the story unifies information from and the experiences of his childhood in an account that transcends limits of either time or place.

King Shuddhodana tried to make Siddhartha abandon the idea of becoming a monk and instead accept a life of ease in the palace; yet despite his father's efforts the prince's understanding of human suffering gradually deepened, and in order to conquer suffering he finally decided to renounce secular life and become a monk. An awareness of the conflicting desires of the two men helps us understand certain occurrences at the time of the birth of Siddhartha's son.

At the time that his wife, Yashodhara, gave birth to their son, Siddhartha was in an outer garden of the palace. Shuddhodana, overjoyed by news of the birth, at once sent a messenger to inform the prince. As soon as he received the message, Siddhartha muttered to himself, "Ah, Rahula is born!" *Rahula* means an obstacle or a bond. It has been suggested that when Siddhartha unconsciously said, "Rahula," he meant that just as he was resolving to renounce the world a bond had been born to obstruct his path.

On learning of Siddhartha's words from the messenger, Shuddhodana was delighted, thinking, "So then, the boy's birth has cooled the prince's ardor to become a monk." And the baby was named Rahula. Much later, Rahula became one of the ten great disciples of the Buddha.

THE GREAT RENUNCIATION   In time King Shuddhodana held a banquet to celebrate the birth of his grandson. His certainty that the boy's birth would prevent Siddhartha from renouncing the world increased his happiness. Siddhartha looked very satisfied, and the king assumed that was because of Rahula; but in truth, Siddhartha's satisfaction stemmed from the fact that he had at last chosen his course: to become a monk even in the face of the king's opposition. In the India of that day, providing an heir to carry on the family line was a major duty—one that a man had to discharge before embarking on a life of religious discipline. Thus although in one sense the birth of Rahula was an obstacle, through the bond linking father and son, in another sense the birth was a release, since it fulfilled Siddhartha's duty to his father and his wife.

It would be wrong, however, to consider only this superficial interpretation of the thoughts of the prince who looked so satisfied that night. Siddhartha was a man like other men, though more sensitive and tender-hearted than others. It must have been unbearable for him to know that would be his last opportunity to see his newborn son; his wife, who was still in childbed; and his father, who at that moment was overjoyed. He dared finally become a monk because he had overcome the unbearable, and his face reflected his joy in this great conquest. This is how I interpret his thinking.

At midnight, Prince Siddhartha mounted his favorite horse, Kanthaka, and accompanied only by his personal servant, Chandaka, he rode forth from the palace. Coming to a beautiful forest at dawn, Siddhartha dismounted and removed his crown and neck ornaments. He then cut off his topknot and changed from his rich garments into coarse clothing.

He asked Chandaka to deliver all his personal ornaments to his foster mother and his wife, saying to the servant, "Give this message to my father, the great king: I do not wish to be reborn in heaven by practicing the virtue of a monk, much less by surrendering to worldly desires. I have renounced the world in order to save all sentient beings from their sufferings. I have seen how they deviate from the right path because of their illusions and how they repeat painful lives. I am determined not to return to the palace until I have attained true enlightenment."

Chandaka, upset by Siddhartha's message for Shuddhodana, threw himself down and cried; but he could not defy the prince, and so he returned to the palace, leading the prince's horse. Thus at the age of twenty-nine Prince Siddhartha became a homeless mendicant, and with a gentle and dignified mien, he entered the forest alone.

Western scholars have named Siddhartha's renunciation of the world the "Great Renunciation." The prince abandoned his royal station for a life of mendicancy. He left a beautiful palace to practice asceticism under trees or on rocks. He shed his fine attire and donned rags. He cast aside great wealth to become an ascetic who, with no more than a begging bowl, wanders in search of the truth. Moreover, he severed the bonds of affection that tied him to his parents, wife, and child. Siddhartha did indeed perform a great renunciation.

Through his great renunciation, Siddhartha was able to attain the perfect wisdom of a buddha. Because the Buddha's perfect wisdom is recorded in his teachings, we of the present day can attain it without having to renounce home, family, or customary way of life. Thanks to the peerless selflessness of Shakyamuni Buddha, we have at our disposal the means to attain profound happiness at the least sacrifice. This is an incomparable gift, and for believers it engenders a debt of gratitude that cannot begin to be repaid. One should not read an account of the life of the Buddha without reflection, as one might be tempted to approach a popular biography or history. Instead, one should contemplate the immeasurable benefits in which all can share today because of the efforts of a single individual some twenty-five hundred years ago.

It is a truism that nothing is gained without sacrifice. We cannot advance in our studies unless we work hard at them. We cannot attain proficiency in a sport unless we sacrifice our leisure time to training. Peace and the stability of society cannot be maintained unless we sacrifice our selfish interests.

Unlike Buddhist priests, monks, or nuns, people who lead ordinary lives do have egoistic attachments, which seem constantly to subside and reassert themselves, because humankind cannot escape a destiny based on the illusion that without egoistic attachment human beings cannot succeed in the struggle for existence. Left alone, our minds will always be filled with egoistic attachment. Through various practices, such as meditation, the reciting of sutras, or invoking the name of Amitabha (the Buddha of the Western Paradise), Buddhists have found it possible to extinguish this egoistic attachment and attain a spiritual state of selflessness. When one achieves such a state of mind, the light of the truth floods one's mind, permeating it.

For the sake of all sentient beings Shakyamuni Buddha renounced all he had, and the greatest of his renunciations was surely his renunciation of self. By freeing himself of both the bonds of the illusion of his own happiness and the desire to be reborn in heaven, he was able to devote the rest of his years to the saving of all sentient beings.

It is said that one who pays dearly gains greatly. This aphorism is apt in both material and spiritual terms. The historical Buddha, who paid dearly to benefit others, attained unsurpassed wisdom, which he left to posterity. We of the present day cannot in turn attain that wisdom without sacrifice. While leading ordinary lives as lay people, we should, insofar as possible, endeavor to renounce our egoistic attachment to self. The greater our renunciation, the greater the happiness we shall gain. I call this the lay believer's renunciation of the world.

From ancient times, many great religious leaders, including Shakyamuni, renounced the world in order to seek a path to salvation for us all, thus relieving us of the hardships of physical renunciation of the world. We have inherited instead an obligation to lead active and productive lives as lay people. We must, however, practice a psychological renunciation; that is, we must renounce egoistic attachment to self. Only when humanity makes this renunciation can it be saved from its sufferings.

THE AUSTERITIES OF THE BODHISATTVA The prince who was to become the historical Buddha has generally been referred to as the Bodhisattva when spoken of during the period of quest and religious disciplines following his great renunciation and up until his enlightenment. A bodhisattva has been described as one who "seeks upward for *bodhi* [wisdom]" and "teaches downward to all beings," that is, one who, on the one hand, perfects himself by aiming at the attainment of enlightenment, but on the other hand, also descends to the level of the unenlightened in order to save them. (In the simplest Mahayana Buddhist terms, a bodhisattva is one who devotes himself to attaining enlightenment not only for himself but for all sentient beings.)

After his renunciation of the secular world the Bodhisattva set out in search of a competent teacher to help him attain enlightenment. Most teachers at that time were ascetics, generally hermit-sages, and the most renowned among them was the hermit-sage Arada-Kalama, who lived in the mountains immediately north of Rajagriha (present-day Rajgir, in the state of Bihar), the capital of the important kingdom of Magadha. The Bodhisattva visited this hermit-sage to learn his method of freeing the spirit from the bonds of the flesh.

Though the philosophy propounded by Arada-Kalama was indeed profound, the Bodhisattva soon understood it and attained the same level of enlightenment as his teacher. Moved by the Bodhisattva's obvious ability,

Arada-Kalama suggested they jointly teach his disciples; but the Bodhisattva declined because he was convinced that he had not yet attained true enlightenment, and he journeyed forth to study under another ascetic.

He next went to the hermit-sage Udraka-Ramaputra, who lived in the mountains near Rajagriha with seven hundred disciples. Udraka-Ramaputra also was a profound philosopher, but the Bodhisattva shortly reached the same state of enlightenment as he and realized that the teachings of Udraka-Ramaputra would not lead him to his goal.

One cannot attain a spiritual state of perfect selflessness through philosophic contemplation alone; and if one does not attain such a state, one cannot comprehend the majesty of the universe, that is, the supreme truth that is capable of saving all sentient beings from their sufferings.

Udraka-Ramaputra proposed that the Bodhisattva join in leading the hermit-sage's disciples, but the Bodhisattva declined Udraka-Ramaputra's offer and once more set out to seek the true path to enlightenment. This time he determined that he would no longer rely on others: he concluded that he could attain enlightenment only through his own practice and meditation.

He went to the southwest and climbed to the top of Mount Gaya, where he sat in meditation, considering what he must do in order to attain enlightenment. From a distance five ascetics, disciples of Udraka-Ramaputra, watched him in his meditation. They had left their teacher, saying among themselves, "We have long studied asceticism under our teacher, yet we have been unable to attain the state of enlightenment preached by him. In a short time, however, that Bodhisattva has completely understood Udraka-Ramaputra's teachings; and finding them insufficient, he now seeks a higher state of wisdom. He is one who will surely attain perfect enlightenment in the future. Let us follow him." Those ascetics, Ajnata-Kaundinya, Bhadrika, Vashpa, Mahanama, and Ashvajit, hold an important place in the history of Buddhism. (According to another version of this story, Shuddhodana had originally sent the five to care for his son; but deeply affected by the Bodhisattva's dedication, they abandoned the secular life to join him.)

Fine forests grew along both banks of the Nairanjana River, near the foot of Mount Gaya; and the rugged Mount Pragbodhi rose on the opposite bank of the river. After the Bodhisattva descended Mount Gaya, he entered the forest near the village of Uruvilva and began to practice ascetic austerities there. With the Bodhisattva's permission, the five ascetics who had followed him joined him in his ascetic practices and also served as his attendants.

Most ascetics at that time practiced various kinds of rigorous self-denial and strict self-discipline. Some sought to attain enlightenment while so severely limiting their food intake that they almost starved. Others immersed themselves in icy waters during the cold season and roasted themselves before blazing fires during the hot season. Some went completely naked, exposed to the extremes of weather in all seasons. One sect believed that ascetics must live where corpses were abandoned and remain silent all their lives. Another required its followers to patiently endure eating grass like a cow and licking the dirt like a dog. Even today in the Hindu holy city of Varanasi (which has also been called Benares), for example, many such ascetics are to be seen. There are those who stand on one leg with one hand raised above their head for long periods, those who lie on beds of thorns or sharp nails, those who hang upside down from tree branches, and those who stare at the sun all day, moving only to follow it through the sky.

It is said that the Bodhisattva engaged in such ascetic practices as controlling his breathing while deep in meditation. One story has it that he disciplined himself to eat but one grain of rice and a single sesame seed each day. An unusual sculpture in the Lahore Museum in Pakistan represents the Bodhisattva during this period of his ascetic practices. This deeply moving image, which dates from the early centuries of the Christian Era, shows his wasted body in a very realistic manner: the protruding bones, the shrunken stomach, and the eyes sunk deeply in his skull indicate the starvation he has undergone. His emaciated face, however, reveals both his benevolent character and his wholehearted dedication to the pursuit of enlightenment.

After six years of ascetic practices, the Bodhisattva realized he could not attain supreme enlightenment through self-mortification because it was mistaken and unnatural. Supreme enlightenment encompasses a path that we can comprehend, a way by which we can understand the universe as it exists and by which we can live in harmony with all things in the universe. Though the extreme discipline of ascetic practices is not without worth when employed as a means of renouncing egoistic attachment to self, one must bear in mind that such self-mortification is but a single step toward true enlightenment. The true path enables us to make the best use of our bodies so long as they are ours. For most people, tormenting the body is a way of tyrannizing the spirit, not freeing it: true freedom of the spirit cannot be achieved through tyranny.

Giving up austerities, the Bodhisattva is said to have

gone to a nearby burning *ghat,* where corpses were cremated, and to have gathered there the ragged, discarded clothing of the dead, which he then washed and donned because it was considered suitable wear for an ascetic. (In those days it was customary to repair such garments by piecing together odd bits of cloth; some say this practice is the origin of Buddhist monks' custom, still practiced today in only slightly altered forms, of making their outer robes by piecing together squares of cloth.)

Clothed thus in rags, the Bodhisattva went to the Nairanjana River, where he shaved off his matted hair and beard and bathed. Afterward he accepted from Sujata, a young woman from the nearby village, a bowl of rice boiled in milk and, mentally and physically refreshed, turned toward a new form of practice.

The Bodhisattva's five followers were deeply disappointed by his actions because they had believed he would surely attain supreme enlightenment, and for that reason they had shared his life during six years of ascetic practices. They thought that he must have eaten the rice gruel because he was no longer able to bear ascetic practices and had failed in his search for enlightenment. They agreed that they should no longer study with him. Dissatisfied and angry, they made their way to Deer Park, outside Varanasi, which was at that time a center for ascetics.

THE TEMPTA-TION OF MARA   The Bodhisattva, taking no notice of the departure of the five ascetics, set out in search of a suitable place to meditate and in so doing climbed Mount Pragbodhi. Near the peak he found a cave that he thought ideal.

Shortly after he entered meditation, the earth quaked violently and the stony cave in which he alone sat became very dangerous. Immediately upon deciding to leave the cave, he became aware of a heavenly voice saying, "There is a Diamond Seat beneath a *bodhi* [wisdom] tree southwest of this place. You should go there for your meditation." Thus he descended the mountain that is now known to us as Pragbodhi, literally, "before wisdom," in commemoration of the historical Buddha's stay there before he achieved enlightenment, or perfect wisdom. The site is now honored by a memorial built by Tibetan priests.

Making his way southwest, the Bodhisattva crossed the Nairanjana River and eventually came upon a large *bodhi* (or bo) tree in the dense forest. Under the tree he found a seat where he could meditate undisturbed. (Since that time the seat, at Bodh Gaya, has been known as the Diamond Seat—the site where the Buddha attained enlightenment.) The Bodhisattva instantly perceived that this was the perfect site for his meditation. Just as he was about to sit, a youth passed by, carrying a basket full of sweet grass on his back. The Bodhisattva thought, "I have been told that, when seeking enlightenment, sages of the past sat on grass spread upon the ground. I will follow their example." He called the boy to him and asked his name. The boy replied that his name was Svastika, literally, "well-being" or "good fortune."

On hearing the boy's name, the Bodhisattva thought their encounter must be a good omen for his attainment of supreme enlightenment. With grass obtained from the youth, the Bodhisattva prepared the seat where he would meditate. It is said that he then vowed: "Even if it means death, I will not rise from this seat until I attain supreme enlightenment."

According to *Shin Shakuson Den* (A New Biography of Shakyamuni) by the late Dr. Shoko Watanabe, a scholar of Indian philosophy who was a professor at Toyo University in Tokyo, the Bodhisattva thought, "In this world of desire, Mara [the Evil One] is master. It is not proper for me to gain unsurpassed, perfect wisdom while Mara is unaware of my attainment. I will summon him. . . . If he sees me becoming a buddha, he too will aspire to perfect wisdom."

We find two important points in this quotation, which may be based on a Sanskrit text. The first is that Mara, the Evil One, did not attempt to attack the Bodhisattva first but the Bodhisattva called out to him. The other is that the Bodhisattva did not set out to vanquish Mara but wanted even him to attain a buddha's enlightenment. These points are early indicators of the fundamentally compassionate nature of Buddhism.

Worried that he would be deprived of his domain if a buddha should appear in and purify his world of desire (whose inhabitants cannot rid themselves of their desires), Mara took steps to protect his world from the Bodhisattva. First, he sent beautiful young women to seduce the Bodhisattva; but the Bodhisattva, unmoved by their enticements, spoke kindly with them about their wrongdoings. The would-be tempters, deeply impressed by the Bodhisattva, returned to Mara and dissuaded the Evil One from persisting in that useless form of attack.

In a rage, Mara next sent a number of demon warriors to the Bodhisattva to force him through violence to submit to the Evil One. Since the Bodhisattva's mind was filled with benevolence, he feared nothing the warriors might do to him, nor did he respond with hostility to their challenges. Mara's warriors were accustomed to overcoming even the most powerful of enemies by force;

but when the Bodhisattva addressed them with compassion, their violence became as futile as beating the air. They could no longer justify their assault on him, and some among the commanders who were sons of the Evil One were forced to turn their thoughts to the virtue of this Bodhisattva.

Mara then changed his strategy and tried to ensnare the Bodhisattva in debate and through cunning confound the Bodhisattva's reasoning abilities. In other words, he attempted to silence the Bodhisattva through intellectual argument; but that effort also failed, and the Evil One at last despaired and desisted. When Mara and his various proxies were thus proved powerless against the virtue of the Bodhisattva, the Bodhisattva's mind was refreshed by the spiritual victory of overcoming all the Evil One's temptations.

Mara first tried to tempt the Bodhisattva through material and sensual desires. He then tried to bend the Bodhisattva to his will through the threat of violence. Finally, the Evil One tried to master the Bodhisattva intellectually. We find ourselves faced with similar challenges today.

The first and second of Mara's temptations are primal, and we meet them in our daily lives. There is no difference between the emotional force of the two, and they exert such strong power because they are so very elemental. Yet human beings, whose passions can be ruled by their minds, can easily reject such enticements. Mara's third temptation, however, is more troubling because of its appeal to the intellect. People who are susceptible to such temptation become so mesmerized that they are deluded by the Evil One's logic, are no longer able to reason for themselves, and readily accept others' statements of what is right. The only defense against this third temptation is to dismiss the logic of the Evil One by relying on religion. I feel strongly that one will not be saved from one's sufferings and society will not improve so long as one neglects to do this.

Mentally refreshed by having overcome the temptations of Mara and his minions, the Bodhisattva had completed the last of the preparatory stages preceding the great turning point in his life.

THE ENLIGHTENMENT The Bodhisattva entered deep meditation and finally attained a spiritual state of perfect selflessness. When human beings attain this state of mind, they become able to see all things in this world as they truly are because their minds have perceived the absolute truth, have been filled with it, and in the end have become one with the truth.

Above all else, the object of the Bodhisattva's practice was humanity's salvation. Because of his right view, he understood how humankind was born and was changed and why it had illusions and sufferings. Various sutras tell us that among the truths on which the Bodhisattva meditated was the teaching we know as the Law of the Twelve Causes, which makes clear that the law of cause and effect lies behind all phenomena and changes in the world. For example, billions of years ago the earth had no life; volcanoes poured forth torrents of lava, and vapor and gas filled the sky. However, when the earth cooled sufficiently and the energy of the lava, vapor, and gas came into contact with the appropriate conditions, or cause, the effect was the birth of microscopic single-celled living creatures. They were produced through the working of this law, which provided the conditions for the generation of life, which eventually, through a long chain of cause and effect, evolved into the life forms we know today. This is but one example of how any phenomenon or change can be analyzed in the light of the Law of the Twelve Causes.

Traditional accounts differ in their reports of the amount of time the Bodhisattva spent in meditation beneath the *bodhi* tree before attaining enlightenment. One account says the period was two weeks; a second holds that it was three weeks; while a third maintains that it was seven weeks. These differences, however, are of no consequence to us. The oldest and most reliable documents state that the Bodhisattva left his father's palace at the age of twenty-nine and attained enlightenment at the age of thirty-five, though there are other accounts that give different ages. Here, too, it does not matter to us which of the records is factually accurate, although the differences may be important to historians or other scholars. Buddhists and students of Buddhism are concerned more with the content of Shakyamuni Buddha's enlightenment and the truths he taught than with establishing the exact dates of events in his life.

Although there is no way of determining the date now, according to Chinese and Japanese Buddhist tradition it was on the morning of December 8, just as the morning star appeared in the sky, when the Bodhisattva's mind was as clear as the breaking day, that he at last attained perfect enlightenment. From that time on his ability to look at all things was different from that of ordinary people. He was able to perceive clearly the real state of all things, unhindered by superficial phenomena: he had gained the eyes of a buddha.

Upon attaining enlightenment he said, "Wonderful! Wonderful! All living beings possess the wisdom and the virtuous sign of the Tathagata [the highest epithet of a buddha], but they do not realize this because of their attachment to desires and illusions."

When Shakyamuni looked on the world through the eyes of a buddha, he noticed that everything appeared completely changed. Animals, plants, and human beings all seemed bathed in such glory and brilliance that it was as if they were pervaded by the same life as the Buddha. His spontaneous "Wonderful! Wonderful!" was uttered out of his great joy at discovering the real state of all existence. The Buddha, however, was not so enraptured by the joy of his unprecedented discovery that he was unmindful of all living beings. He immediately observed their actual states and perceived the cause of their sufferings: their attachment to desires and illusions.

It is impossible for an ordinary human being to fully comprehend the profundity of Shakyamuni's enlightenment or the magnitude of his discoveries upon attaining enlightenment, but we can recognize the depth of his experiences when we read his subsequent teachings. For example, Shakyamuni's unequalled insight is apparent in "Tactfulness," chapter 2 of the Lotus Sutra, in his explanation of the reason that human beings repeat their sufferings and their struggles with one another.

> "I, observing with the Buddha's eyes,
> See the creatures in the six states of existence,
> Poor and without happiness and wisdom,
> In the dangerous path of mortality,
> In continuous, unending misery,
> Firmly fettered by the five desires
> Like the yak caring for its tail,
> Smothered by greed and infatuation,
> Blinded and seeing nothing;
> They seek not the Buddha, the mighty,

And the Law to end sufferings,
But deeply [fall] into heresies,
And seek by suffering to be rid of suffering.
For the sake of all these creatures,
My heart is stirred with great pity."

In Shakyamuni's time yaks, which are said to devote much time to the grooming of their silken-haired tails, were often fated to die at the hands of men seeking only the luxuriant tails as prized ornaments. In a similar way human beings, who through the five senses are also deeply attached to their bodies and physical desires, cannot perceive the truth and continue to be worried by their sufferings.

DECIDING TO PREACH In the portion of "Tactfulness" that I quoted above, Shakyamuni continues with a description of his thoughts after attaining the perfect wisdom—supreme enlightenment—of a buddha.

"When I first sat on the wisdom throne,
Looking at [that] tree and walking about it
During thrice seven days,
I pondered such matters as these:
'The wisdom which I have obtained
Is wonderful and supreme.
[But] all creatures are dull in their capacities,
Pleasure-attached and blind with ignorance.
Such classes of beings as these,
[I saw,] how can they be saved?'
Thereupon all the Brahma kings
And Lord Shakra of all the gods,

The four heavenly beings who protect the worlds,
Also the god Great Sovereign
And all the other heavenly beings,
With hundreds of thousands of myriads of followers,
Respectfully saluted with folded hands,
Entreating me to roll the wheel of the Law.
Then I pondered within myself:
'If I only extol the Buddha-vehicle,
All creatures, being sunk in suffering,
Will not be able to believe this Law,
And by breaking the Law through unbelief
Will fall into the three evil paths.
I had rather not preach the Law,
But instantly enter nirvana.'
Then, on remembering what former buddhas
Performed by their tactful powers,
[I thought:] 'The Way which I have now attained
I must preach as the tripartite vehicle.' "

The words "former buddhas" here are important. In other sutras Shakyamuni said of his enlightenment, "I was awakened to the unparalleled truth and possessed the wisdom of the Tathagata [one who has reached the truth and come to declare it]." Afterward he proceeded with his preaching, saying, "I discovered the old path trod by those who in the past had gained the Tathagata's righteous wisdom." In the Lotus Sutra, he also says, "Only a buddha together with a buddha can fathom the Reality of All Existence."

Shakyamuni never claimed that the truth he had perceived was original with him. He reasoned that the absolute truth exists eternally and must have been perceived many times before, and he declared that he had simply discovered the same truth known in the past by those who had attained the Tathagata's peerless wisdom. We can but admire the spirit in which he renounced all self-assertion and esteemed only the truth. In these days, when so many people seem to have become the incarnation of self-interest, it is good for us to recall the example set by Shakyamuni, who did not regard his enlightenment as unique to himself.

When Shakyamuni said, "Then, on remembering what former buddhas / Performed by their tactful powers," he meant that there had been many people in the past who had perceived the universal truth and that they had not taught it baldly, precisely as they had perceived it, but that they had taught with great tact, preaching the truth to ordinary people in various ways, according to each person's power and level of understanding.

Turning next to the actual situation of ordinary people, Shakyamuni found that many were prey to desires and illusions but others were not corrupted by desires and illusions, just as the lotus, though growing in a bog, brings forth a pure, beautiful flower unsullied by the mud. Shakyamuni concluded, "Those people who have not been corrupted will be able to understand supreme enlightenment if a suitable method of teaching is used. Very well, I will preach to them." To Brahma, chief among the Hindu deities, who had pleaded earnestly with Shakyamuni to bring his truth and salvation to the world, Shakyamuni said, "I will accede to your entreaties and will bring my teaching to all living beings, like a rain of nectar. All living beings in the world! All those, including gods, men, and devils, who have ears! Come to me and hear this Law."

The instant of Shakyamuni's utterance is a very precious one because it was then that the doctrine of the

Buddha was born in this world. At that moment this doctrine—which has continued to spread throughout the world for some twenty-five hundred years, reviving the spirit as rain revives parched soil—took shape in Shakyamuni's mind.

The immense stupa of the Mahabodhi Temple at Bodh Gaya, where Shakyamuni attained enlightenment, can be seen from a great distance. The moving sight of that stupa soaring high above the surrounding plain suggests to us the reason that the ancients built imposing stupas to honor the Buddha's virtue. The dignity of the great stupa at Bodh Gaya eclipses the other structures nearby. The precincts of the temple lie in a slight depression about halfway up a thickly wooded hill. One can walk completely around the stupa, as is the case at most holy sites in India, where it has long been the custom to worship enshrined relics by walking clockwise around a stupa three or seven times.

The great stupa faces east, and a massive bo, or *bodhi,* tree stands behind it, to the west. Beneath the tree, a huge footed, carved stone slab—the Diamond Seat— marks what is believed to be the spot where Shakyamuni sat in meditation and attained enlightenment. Set into the stupa wall facing this seat is a statue of Shakyamuni seated with his left hand resting palm up in his lap and his right hand, fingers extended toward the earth, resting palm down on his right knee, in the mudra of subduing the Evil One. Set along the north wall of the stupa, about one meter from the foundation, are *chankramana* stones (literally, "walking about after meditation" stones). Legend holds that lotus flowers sprang up in the footprints left by the Buddha as he walked around the bo tree during the first two weeks after his enlightenment. Because of the auspicious generation of flowers in this legend, believers in later ages laid bricks in what they supposed were the Buddha's footprints, and atop the bricks they placed stones in which lotus blossoms had been engraved.

On a hillock at the east end of the path beside the *chankramana* stones stands a white stupa called the Tree-Viewing Stupa. Because of the statement "Looking at [that] tree and walking about it / During thrice seven days" in the portion of chapter 2 of the Lotus Sutra quoted above, it is believed that Shakyamuni remained near the site of this stupa during the third week following his enlightenment, meditating and contemplating the bo tree as an expression of gratitude to the tree that had sheltered him as he meditated until attaining enlightenment. At the northern boundary of the temple precincts stands another stupa, marking the site where Shakyamuni is said to have meditated during the fourth week after his enlightenment. One story told of that period says that at that time his body emitted light of five colors (green, yellow, red, white, and orange), and the rays were cast on the bo tree.

Regardless of any embellishments added to the accounts in the early centuries after the Buddha's death, study of the Buddha's own narrative as recorded in various sutras convinces us that he spent the first several weeks following his enlightenment in the vicinity of the bo tree at Bodh Gaya meditating on how to teach the profound truth that he had realized.

2 · Rolling the Wheel of the Law

TO DEER PARK   Concerning his meditation after enlightenment and his decision to teach, in "Tactfulness" the Buddha himself says,

"[I] again reflected thus:
'Having come forth into the disturbed and evil world,
I, according to the buddhas' behest,
Will also obediently proceed.'
Having finished pondering this matter,
I instantly went to Varanasi."

Here the Buddha is saying, "I came forth into this disturbed and evil world charged with the mission of saving it." Buddhists always remember the Buddha's resoluteness and great compassion for all living beings, which must be regarded not merely as expressions of the Buddha's personal concern for us but as the real concerns of all humankind. Even if we feel that we are as yet very far from achieving the spiritual development of the Buddha, we must strive to accomplish the mission entrusted to us as ordinary people.

Undoubtedly, during the several weeks that he remained at Bodh Gaya in meditation and thought following his enlightenment, the Buddha devoted much time to organizing the teachings he would present in explaining the profound truth to which he had been enlightened. When he at last felt fully prepared, the Buddha departed on the teaching mission that would bring his message to others.

On beginning his mission Shakyamuni thought, "To whom should I first preach this Law? Who will be able to understand it?" His former teachers, Arada-Kalama and Udraka-Ramaputra, came to mind; but he learned that the two hermit-sages were already dead. He then remembered the five ascetics who had practiced austerities with him and later, becoming disillusioned, had left him. He was told that they were staying at Deer Park, near Varanasi, where many hermits gathered for ascetic practices. Alone, Shakyamuni made his way on foot to Varanasi, over two hundred kilometers to the west of Bodh Gaya.

Shortly after leaving Bodh Gaya, Shakyamuni encountered a young monk who addressed him, saying, "You look purified. Under whom have you studied in becoming a monk? To what kind of teaching have you devoted yourself?" Shakyamuni replied with quiet dignity, "I am all-wise, a victor over all things. I have extinguished all desires and become detached from all things. Able to attain enlightenment unaided, I have no teacher and no equal in this world. I am a buddha." The monk said, "That may be so," and briskly resumed his course.

That young monk, Upaka by name, is still remembered today because, by not asking to be instructed, he lost the opportunity to be the first to hear Shakyamuni's message. Anyone who seeks after the Way must regard all people with whom he comes into contact as teachers and all places as proper places in which to learn the truth. For example, the Flower Garland Sutra contains the story of a monk called Sudhana-shreshthidaraka, who was able to learn a valuable lesson from a prostitute. Thus Upaka, who was immediately moved by the serene dignity of the Buddha, ought to have respectfully asked Shakyamuni to explain his enlightenment. Upaka was later to regret sorely that he had not done so, and he did eventually accept the teachings of the Buddha.

THE FIRST SERMON   After walking many days across the hot plains of India, Shakyamuni finally reached Varanasi. He soon went to Deer Park, where the five ascetics who had accompanied him for six years were then staying.

Seeing a monk approaching, the five recognized him as the Gautama whom they had followed in his practice of austerities (Gautama was Shakyamuni's family name). "That is Gautama, isn't it? He is the fallen monk who failed in his ascetic practices. Let us refrain from paying our respects to him when he comes to us. However, we may give him some food. . . ."

Though they spoke thus to one another, when they met Shakyamuni they were so affected by his dignity that they were incapable of remaining indifferent. Each rose unconsciously and received him reverently, making obeisance to him. They took his begging bowl, washed his feet and dried them, and prepared a seat of honor for him. They greeted him: "Our friend, Gautama!"

Lumbini Garden, the birthplace of Shakyamuni Buddha.

Piprahwa, India, believed to be the site of the ancient city of Kapilavastu.

The great stupa at Bodh Gaya, where Shakyamuni attained enlightenment. ▶

The Diamond Seat at Bodh Gaya, which marks what is believed to be the spot where Shakyamuni sat in meditation until attaining enlightenment. The bo tree is said to be the fourth planted on this site since the enlightenment.

Photo by Isamu Maruyama

◀ *Deer Park at Sarnath, near Varanasi, where Shakyamuni preached his first sermon after attaining enlightenment.*

The site atop Vulture Peak where Shakyamuni often preached.

The remains of the house of the Shravasti merchant Sudatta, who purchased the land for the Jetavana Monastery by covering it with gold.

The Jetavana Monastery, near Shravasti, which was presented to Shakyamuni by the merchant Sudatta and Prince Jeta.

The site in the shala grove at Kushinagara where Shakyamuni is believed to have died.

The mound built at the site of Shakyamuni's cremation.

The urn from Piprahwa that contained the Buddha's relics. The inscription reads: "This is the urn of the relics of the Bhagavat, the Buddha of the Shakya tribe, that is enshrined (by honorable brothers and sisters, wives and children)."

Shakyamuni then solemnly declared: "You must no longer address me as Gautama, nor yet as friend. I have already become a buddha. I will preach to you the eternal truth I have perceived. If you practice this according to my teaching, you will surely attain enlightenment and achieve your purpose in becoming monks."

Anyone other than Shakyamuni making such a seemingly haughty statement, so similar to his declaration to Upaka, would have inevitably invited accusations of arrogance. It is not possible for the ordinary human mind to encompass Shakyamuni's own comprehension of his buddhahood. His awareness was founded both in the universal truth to which he had been awakened and in his realization that all things of heaven and earth were his responsibility. His announcement would have been astounding without his confident affirmation "I am a buddha."

Those who linger at the various stages before attaining buddhahood are yet unperfected and imprudent and therefore should always be modest. However, since Shakyamuni was a buddha, any reticence on his part would have denigrated his buddhahood. We must understand this point in order to appreciate that Shakyamuni was speaking forthrightly, not exhibiting overweening pride.

The five monks were inspired by Shakyamuni's virtuous mien and paid him homage despite their initial reaction, but they did not consent immediately to listen to Shakyamuni's teaching. In fact, at first they did not want to hear it. However, Shakyamuni, ardently desiring to enlighten them, addressed them three times, saying, "I will now preach the Law to you. Come and listen to me." Three times they refused to heed him. Finally he said to them sternly, "Monks! Have I ever spoken untruthfully to you? Have I?" They recalled that he had always taught them with honesty, and they were moved by his compassionate wish to save all sentient beings from their sufferings. As they reflected on these things, a desire to hear Shakyamuni's message gradually arose in them.

Shakyamuni had reached Deer Park in the afternoon, and he spent the hours from early evening onward alone in silent meditation. At midnight, when the sounds of the day had died away, a serene air stole upon the surroundings and Shakyamuni at last began to preach his epochal sermon.

"Monks! In this world there are two extremes—that of self-mortification and that of self-indulgence—that must be avoided. By avoiding these two extremes and following the Middle Path, I have attained the highest enlightenment." Thus Shakyamuni began his first sermon.

He then preached the Four Noble Truths, teaching that man must recognize that life is filled with suffering (the Truth of Suffering), grasp the real cause of suffering (the Truth of Cause), and by daily religious practice (the Truth of the Path) extinguish all kinds of suffering (the Truth of Extinction). Shakyamuni went on to expound the Eightfold Path—right view, right thinking, right speech, right action, right living, right endeavor, right memory, and right meditation—as the Truth of the Path leading to the extinction of all suffering. First Ajnata-Kaundinya and then each of the other *bhikshus,* or monks, reached the first stage of enlightenment, becoming free of all illusions. Speaking of this first sermon Shakyamuni says, in chapter 2 of the Lotus Sutra,

"The nirvana-nature of all existence,
Which is inexpressible,
I by [my] tactful ability

Preached to the five *bhikshus*.
This is called [the first] rolling of the Law-wheel,
Whereupon there was the news of nirvana
And also the separate names of *Arhat,*
Of Law, and of Sangha."

The expression "rolling of the Law-wheel" requires some explanation. In Indian mythology the ideal ruler, known as a wheel-rolling king, was supposed to govern by rolling a wheel and to rule not by armed might but by virtue. In Buddhist terms there are four such kings, each with a precious wheel of gold, silver, copper, or iron, in accordance with how large a portion of the world he rules. The king of the gold wheel unites and rules the entire world.

The Buddha's Law is like the wheel of gold. When a great sage preaches this Law it is as if he had rolled the gold wheel: all come to respect and honor him and his rule, or teaching. Thus "to roll the Law-wheel," or the "wheel of the Law," means to teach the Buddha's Law.

During the forty-five years between his first sermon and his death, Shakyamuni ceaselessly rolled the Law-wheel in the villages and countries of northern and central India, and that Law-wheel continued to roll even after his death. In one direction, it rolled through Central Asia into China and Korea and on to Japan; in another direction, it rolled throughout Southeast Asia.

FORMING THE SANGHA Further explanation of the phrase "And also the separate names of *Arhat*, / Of Law, and of Sangha," quoted above, is needed here. An *arhat*, literally, "man of worth, honorable one," is an enlightened person who is free from all cravings, and thus from rebirth, and is therefore worthy of the respect of all who meet him. For a time after his enlightenment Shakyamuni was the only *arhat;* but after the first rolling of the Law-wheel, when the truth to which Shakyamuni had been enlightened was first made known to others, five more *arhats* joined him. The Sangha, or community of believers, did not exist before his first sermon but came into being when the five monks who had attained enlightenment became his disciples. In terms of the Three Treasures—the Buddha, the Law, and the Sangha—Shakyamuni was at first the embodiment of all three. It was not until after the first rolling of the wheel of the Law that the Buddha, the Law, and the Sangha acquired separate identities.

After delivering his first sermon, Shakyamuni decided to remain at Varanasi with his five disciples during the rainy season, which was about to begin. Living in Varanasi, an important trade and commercial center, was a wealthy merchant called Kulika who had a son named Yashas. Kulika loved his only son so much that he built summer and winter villas for Yashas and had many beautiful maidens wait upon him, clothing him in gorgeous raiment and putting golden shoes on his feet.

Once Yashas chanced to waken from a deep sleep at midnight after having entertained a number of friends and their wives. He called out to his serving women for water, but none awoke at his summons. Going to fetch some water, Yashas passed the women's sleeping quarters. His dancers and serving women appeared to have been exhausted by the party, for they lay about wherever they had fallen asleep rather than in their accustomed places. Awake, the maidens seemed beautiful, gentle, and charming; but asleep they were a disagreeable sight, with spittle dribbling from their open mouths and their no longer graceful limbs flung carelessly in all directions.

Disenchanted by the disordered postures of his servants, Yashas was rendered speechless. He felt great contempt for himself for having indulged in pleasures with those young women. Despite the late hour he rushed from the house and walked about the city as if mad, crying, "Ah me! How miserable I am! How distressed I am!" Without thinking, he made his way to Deer Park.

As the eastern sky was beginning to turn gray, Shakyamuni arose to meditate while strolling through the park. Yashas, who met him there, immediately recognized Shakyamuni as a peerless sage. He said beseechingly, "Master of the precepts! I am deeply anguished. Please save me!"

Shakyamuni answered tenderly, "Do not worry so about your distress. At my side there is no more sorrow or pain. Sit here and listen to what I tell you now."

He then taught Yashas that human life was all suffering but that there was a way to extinguish that suffering. Yashas became enlightened to a way of viewing the world that was completely different from the way in which he had viewed it in the past, and he suddenly felt unburdened. Shedding his rich garments, he made a request of Shakyamuni: "Please permit me to become one of your disciples." Shakyamuni, recognizing the purity of Yashas's mind, accepted him as a disciple. Thus the seventh *arhat* appeared in this world.

The house of the merchant Kulika was in great turmoil when the disappearance of Yashas was discovered. Kulika sent his many servants to look everywhere for his lost son and, becoming distraught, himself set out in search of some trace of Yashas.

Shakyamuni, observing Kulika at Deer Park in quest of his missing son, called out, saying, "Merchant Kulika!

You need not feel concern for your son, Yashas, whom you seek. You will see him before long. Sit here for a little while and listen to what I tell you now."

Using various examples and methods, Shakyamuni instructed the rich merchant on the suffering of life and the way to overcome that suffering. When he perceived that Kulika was free of his attachment to his family and to material things and that he had accepted the Buddhist way of viewing life, Shakyamuni allowed him to meet with Yashas, who had been hidden close by.

Kulika, having been awakened to Shakyamuni's teachings, was not surprised to see his son wearing the simple robe of a monk and said to Yashas, "It is fitting that you have become a monk. Thanks to you, I have been able to have my eyes opened to the great truth preached by the World-honored One. Hereafter I also will follow his teachings as a layman." Kulika then addressed Shakyamuni: "I will devote myself to you, World-honored One, to your teachings, and to your followers. Please accept me as one of your believers." Shakyamuni accepted him at once.

Kulika invited Shakyamuni and Yashas to dine at his home on the following day and asked if Shakyamuni would deliver a sermon at that time. After listening to Shakyamuni the next day, both Yashas's mother and his wife became devoted to the Buddha's teachings. Thus, in the space of two days, two new words—*upasaka*, meaning a male lay believer, and *upasika*, meaning a female lay believer—entered the vocabulary of Buddhism. We should bear in mind that in India at that time women were regarded as naturally impure and lustful beings who would distract a man from serious religious study, and thus they were not permitted to join religious communities. Yet Shakyamuni paid no heed to such beliefs and gladly included both female lay believers and nuns among his followers. Because of that practice we know he truly believed in the equality of all human beings.

Among Yashas's friends in Varanasi were four to whom he was especially close. When they heard that Yashas, whose opinion they respected, had become a monk and that his whole family had become lay followers of the Buddha, they yearned to be instructed by the Buddha. Upon hearing his teachings they requested to be allowed to follow him as monks. Learning of the actions of Yashas and the four friends, fifty other friends of Yashas came to listen to Shakyamuni and also asked for permission to become monks. All these friends of Yashas became free of all illusions and ultimately attained the enlightenment of an *arhat*. By this time, including the five ascetics, the community of monks, or the Sangha, numbered sixty, all *arhats*.

When his disciples numbered sixty, Shakyamuni thought it was at last time to begin his teaching mission, carrying to as many people as possible his message and the profound truth to which he had been enlightened. He spoke to his disciples: "Monks! I have now freed myself from all attachment to the world. You also have emancipated yourselves from all bonds. Therefore, let us go out to teach others for the sake of the peace and the happiness of humankind. But you must not go together on the same way. Each of you must choose a different road and thus preach this Law widely. I will take the road to Rajagriha [the capital of Magadha]."

Brahmanism, the major Indian religion at that time, made no effort to disseminate its teachings. Members of the priestly caste, the Brahmans, were responsible for its religious rites and prayers: the worship of members of other castes consisted chiefly of private prayer and of making offerings, which the priests would, with the proper ritual, present to the gods on behalf of the supplicant. Members of the lowest caste, the Shudras, who were slaves or laborers, were not permitted to profess belief in Brahmanism. Given such social conditions, the efforts of Shakyamuni to bring enlightenment equally to all people, both highborn and low, must have seemed nothing short of revolutionary, although in the light of our present-day views on the role of religion, we regard his course as only proper.

THE THREE TREASURES   When Shakyamuni first began his teaching ministry, he met personally with every man who wished to become a monk and himself gave permission for the man to join the Sangha; but once Shakyamuni and his disciples set out on their separate journeys, it would have been impossible for him to meet each aspiring monk. To bring enlightenment to as great a number of people as possible, Shakyamuni decided that his indirect permission could be given to those who desired to become monks after hearing his message from his disciples. Yet permission could not be granted indiscriminately to all those who sought it: only those with a sincere resolve and who were spiritually ready could be accepted. Shakyamuni therefore taught his disciples the three basic elements that are the spiritual foundation of Buddhism—the Buddha, the Law, and the Sangha. Shakyamuni felt that anyone who placed faith in these three elements, known as the Three Treasures, would be able to become his disciple without receiving permission directly from him. Today believers still use the following formula to express their faith in the Three Treasures.

We take refuge in the Buddha.
We take refuge in the Law.
We take refuge in the Sangha.

These words mean: "We depend on the Buddha, the truth preached by him, and the community of like-minded people united in their belief in and practice of his teachings, and we devote ourselves to these Three Treasures." Shakyamuni taught these three elements to his followers because he knew that without a foundation on which they could depend spiritually they would be unable to believe and faithfully practice his teachings.

It is interesting to note that much of Japan's first law code, the Seventeen-Article Constitution promulgated in A.D. 604 by Prince-Regent Shotoku, was based on the spirit of Mahayana Buddhism as transmitted in the Lotus Sutra. For example, Article 2 of that constitution reads: "Sincerely reverence the Three Treasures. . . . What man in what age can fail to reverence this Law? Few men are utterly bad. They may be taught to follow it. But if they do not betake them to the Three Treasures, wherewithal shall their crookedness be made straight?"

Buddhism teaches that we must take refuge in the Three Treasures if we are to create a better society, and even non-Buddhists can accept this belief if we understand the Three Treasures in their broadest sense as a great teacher, a correct teaching preached by that teacher, and a community of believers in that teaching. Prince-Regent Shotoku undoubtedly had this Buddhist principle in mind when he included in his constitution the exhortation "Sincerely reverence the Three Treasures."

The Buddha in whom Buddhists must take refuge is

the Lord Shakyamuni; the Law they must follow is the Buddha's teachings; and the Sangha to which they must belong is the community of people who share their faith. At the same time, however, Buddhists must also transmit the fundamental spirit of the Three Treasures in a much broader sense.

The Buddha should be understood as the great life-force of the universe, the fundamental force and truth that is the source of all existences. Therefore, "take refuge in the Buddha" means to devote oneself to this great life-force of the universe and to attain a state of spiritual unity with it. A person who can achieve that state of mind and continuously maintain that mental attitude lives in the ultimate world of awakening and enjoys the highest and freest state of mind that a human being can attain. When taking refuge in the Buddha is understood in this general sense, non-Buddhists also can embrace it.

In a similar manner, when the phrase "take refuge in the Law" is understood in a broad sense, it means to obey reason, to live in accordance with the Law or truth of the universe. This is the best and most correct way for us to live, since we do not sin, nor are we at a loss as to how to think or act because we know the Law, the correct way of life.

Since modern society is still imperfect, a person who lives in accord with the truth may be thought by others to be temporarily reduced to an unhappy state. Such a person may seem to be unhappy, but properly speaking, he is not unhappy because he is in fact a vital part of the foundation on which a more harmonious world will be built; such a person should be regarded as a very precious being.

When we say that human beings should live in accordance with the Law and the truth of the universe, some people complain that they do not know how to go about this because the guidelines for such a way of life are very vague. However, in following this way of life we can dispense with detailed methodology. Through belief one can naturally live in such a way and attain such a state of mind as to completely abandon one's ego.

People living not as monks or nuns but as ordinary lay believers may find it impossible to renounce their egos completely. But if they can free themselves from their egos for even one hour of the day through such religious practice as sutra recitation or meditation, they will find that practice exerts a good influence on their lives during the remaining twenty-three hours. A person who continues this practice for many years will automatically live a good life and become united with the fundamental truth. This illustrates the fundamental meaning of taking refuge in the Law, which is a concept that can be approved of by people everywhere, regardless of their religious beliefs.

The phrase "take refuge in the Sangha" expresses devotion to the third of the Three Treasures. Shakyamuni called his religious community the Sangha (literally, a "group or union") because he regarded harmony among believers as a requisite for the formation of a community. In speculating on Shakyamuni's thoughts, we may well imagine that he cherished the belief that harmony is the indispensable requisite of any human society. Shakyamuni's true intent therefore may have been for believers to take refuge in the virtue of harmony. The words of the formula must have been rooted in a strong desire to see all human beings unite in concord, for we find this very thought recorded in various sutras preached by Shakyamuni.

All human beings lovingly united with one another and harmoniously following the course of perpetual spiritual growth—this important aspiration is the ideal of thoughtful people everywhere. In order to realize this ideal, we must begin by making even our smallest relationships harmonious. We must begin by harmonizing our bonds with family, friends, and associates and then gradually extend our efforts to the whole of society. We can point to the Sangha as the most telling example of many strangers lovingly, harmoniously uniting with one another. Because the Sangha, a community of people united closely through their belief in the same religion, is not consecrated to worldly affairs, it is an ideal instrument for bringing harmony to people. Regardless of what religion we follow, when we become part of a Sangha we make use of the most effective and fitting means of establishing the foundation that will bring our spirits into harmony with all human beings.

In a general sense, to take refuge in the Sangha means to respect harmony as the basis of human society, to depend upon it, to devote ourselves to it, and to endeavor to realize it. Anyone should be able to understand and accept this broad interpretation of taking refuge in the Sangha.

The significance of devotion to the Three Treasures, which I have outlined here, is obviously something of worth both to Buddhists and to people of other faiths. I believe that Buddhists must not only take refuge in the Three Treasures in the traditional Buddhist sense but also devote themselves to the Three Treasures in their broadest meaning. In that way the true spirit of Buddhism can be shared with all the world's people.

3 · The Teaching Mission

TO MAGADHA The sixty *arhats* of Shakyamuni's Sangha, or community, started out on their teaching journeys while Shakyamuni went east to Magadha alone. Its capital, Rajagriha, was not far from the village of Uruvilva, near which Shakyamuni had practiced austerities and also near which was the bo tree under which he had attained enlightenment. Many sages and religious teachers and their disciples were then living in and around Rajagriha, and it was to those men that Shakyamuni wished to preach.

When Shakyamuni had first gone to Rajagriha to study under the hermit-sage Arada-Kalama, all the townspeople viewed with wonder the unknown ascetic who possessed such nobility and dignity though he wore only a poor robe. Rumor had it that the monk was Prince Siddhartha of the Shakyas, who had left his father's palace for a religious life, and all Rajagriha was astir with people who wished to see him.

Becoming aware of the people's excitement, King

Bimbisara asked one of his retainers the cause. The man replied, "Your Majesty, I think you have heard something of Prince Siddhartha of the Shakyas. When he was but an infant in Kapilavastu, it was predicted: 'If he remains in the palace to succeed to the throne, he will become a great king who rules all the world. But if he forsakes his throne to enter the religious life, he will become an unparalleled great sage.' That Prince Siddhartha is now staying here."

On hearing this, the king decided to meet Prince Siddhartha. Although Magadha was at that time a prosperous and powerful country, Bimbisara wanted to increase its power and to annex the country of Kaushala to the northwest, across the Ganges; and he felt the need of a counselor of undisputed virtue to assist him in realizing his ambitions. The king thought that a prince of whom it had been prophesied that he would become a great king ruling all the world would be a perfect adviser. Bimbisara supposed that the prince had left his father's palace to become an ascetic because he was discontent with his father's unwillingness to step down from the throne. Such an assumption was not unreasonable in the India of that day, for much of ancient Indian history revolves around bitter struggles that pitted father against son and brother against brother in attempts to gain a throne or political ascendancy.

Bimbisara went to the mountains outside Rajagriha, where he found the prince seated on a boulder, meditating. Immediately feeling admiration for the prince, the king bowed politely and said, "I am Bimbisara, king of this country. I am told that you are the heir to a throne. Why have you forsaken such an exalted station to become a monk? If you have renounced the world only because your father would not abdicate the throne in

your favor, I will give half of this country to you. If you
are not satisfied with half, I will not hesitate to give you
the whole country. Because I have a powerful army, I
am certain that I shall conquer many countries and become a great king. Will you not join me?"

The prince answered softly and evenly, "Great king, I
sincerely thank you for your kind offer, but I am a monk
who has already abandoned all worldly desires. I seek
only the way of freedom from the bonds of illusion and
suffering. Great king, please dismiss me from your mind.
May you rule your country rightly, ensuring that the
people live in peace."

Hearing the prince's reply, the king's respect deepened, and he said, "I understand well. I will not press
you, but I have a request to make of you. When you
reach your goal and attain enlightenment, please come
here again and lead me to enlightenment." The prince
willingly agreed to the king's request.

Because of that promise to King Bimbisara, Shakyamuni chose to go to Magadha to preach his path to enlightenment.

On his way to Magadha Shakyamuni encountered thirty
young men, whom he enlightened. As the story is usually
told, Shakyamuni was meditating under a tree in a
forest when a large group of young men rushed to him,
saying, "Sage, have you just now seen a young woman
pass by here?"

Calmly opening his half-closed eyes, Shakyamuni said,
"No, I have not seen such a woman. Why do you seek
her?"

"She has run away with our clothing and jewels."
They then told him their story.

The thirty, who were all of royal blood, enjoyed going

on outings together with their wives. This day they had come to the forest and dined. One of the young men was unmarried, and a prostitute had accompanied him. After eating and drinking heavily, they had all taken a short nap; and while they slept, the prostitute had stolen their valuables and disappeared.

After hearing their story, Shakyamuni asked them gently, "Which do you think more important, to seek that woman or to seek yourselves?"

Looking unsurely at one another, the young men were unable to answer his question immediately and asked, "What do you mean by that?"

"My question is this: Which is more important, the young woman or yourselves?"

Startled by Shakyamuni's words, the young men realized they were being asked a very serious question and assumed a respectful attitude. "O Sage, we think it is more important to seek ourselves."

"This you have understood well. Now sit there, all of you, and I will teach you the Law whereby to seek yourselves." Shakyamuni then taught them in plain words about the fundamental problem of human life. Because they were all well educated they quickly understood the true nature of human life, attaining the initial stage of enlightenment, and they requested to be allowed to become Shakyamuni's disciples.

Although this story relates but a single episode in Shakyamuni's long life, it does illustrate two very important points. The first is Shakyamuni's tactful method of teaching. Tactfulness adapts the teaching so that it suits both the needs and understanding of particular people and the circumstances. Tactful teaching is individualized teaching of the fundamental truth. Another example of this is to be found in the account of an incident that occurred much later.

Once when Shakyamuni was staying in Kaushala at the Jetavana Monastery, which had been built near the town of Shravasti by the merchant Sudatta, a woman half-crazed by her child's death was wandering about the town carrying the dead child in her arms, seeking a medicine that would revive it. Observing the woman's misery, Shakyamuni said to her, "I have something precious to teach you, but first bring me a poppy seed from a house that death has never entered." After searching throughout the town, the woman found there was not a single house that death had not visited. When she realized that all human beings are mortal, she returned to her senses as if awakening from a dream. If we compare the story of this woman with that of the young men, we can appreciate Shakyamuni's superb skill in guiding people according to their needs.

In the case of the young men, he saw at once that they were of good family and well educated. Therefore he could tell them straightforwardly to search for themselves, and although surprised by his directness, they were able to reflect on their conduct and the meaning of human life. Then Shakyamuni could give them a detailed explanation of the meaning of life. But the woman of Shravasti was young and uneducated. Hence he asked her to search for a poppy seed and thus led her to discover for herself how mistaken she was.

It has been said that the Buddha should be admired not only as a supreme man of religion but also as an excellent educator. I too subscribe to this view. As a teacher of humanity, Shakyamuni devoted his life to leading innumerable people to the path of truth in ac-

cordance with each person's intellectual ability, character, and circumstances. The great teacher Shakyamuni
had mastered this method of preaching.

The second point to be learned from the story of the
enlightenment of the thirty young men, as well as from
the story of the woman of Shravasti, is Shakyamuni's
attitude toward preaching the Law. He did not preach
and guide as a formal ritual but instead regarded everyday situations as proper settings for teaching and enlightening. He preached the Law in any place, at any
time, and to any person.

In chapter 5 of the Lotus Sutra, "The Parable of the
Herbs," he discloses the general vows of the Buddha:
"Those who have not yet been saved I cause to be saved;
those who have not yet been set free to be set free; those
who have not yet been comforted to be comforted;
those who have not yet obtained nirvana to obtain nirvana."

Having sworn those great vows, the Buddha promptly
succored those who were suffering. When he encountered
people who had been enslaved by their illusions, he was
compelled to free them from their illusions at once. He
could not refrain from instantly teaching the path of
liberation to those who had not known it. In other ages,
however, many men of religion have taught only at spe-
cific places, such as temples, or on formal occasions, such
as religious gatherings. Looking back on Shakyamuni's
attitude toward expounding his teachings, we realize how
mistaken such professional preachers have been.

In the Sutra of the Great Decease, which contains his
final sermon, Shakyamuni said, "This teaching shall be
entrusted not to *bhikshus* [monks] and *bhikshunis* [nuns]
but to *upasakas* [laymen] and *upasikas* [laywomen]." He
must have had many reasons for entrusting his teaching

to laymen and laywomen, and surely one of them was that lay believers have so many opportunities to enlighten others in everyday situations. But if Buddhists do not make use of every opportunity to share the compassionate teachings of the Buddha with as many people as possible, they cannot expect to bring peace to the world.

When we consider Shakyamuni's trust in lay believers and his attitude toward the thirty young men he met in the forest, we see that the attitude one ought to maintain in doing any religious work is clear: one should emulate Shakyamuni and strive to be both understanding and pragmatic.

THE KASHYAPA BROTHERS AND THE SERMON ON BURNING

Living in the vicinity of Rajagriha were three renowned ascetics, brothers from a Brahman family: Uruvilva-Kashyapa, Nadi-Kashyapa, and Gaya-Kashyapa. The eldest of the three, Uruvilva-Kashyapa, is said to have been one hundred and twenty years old, and the other brothers are also said to have been more than one hundred years old. The three brothers were possessed of supernatural powers and had great influence on their followers, among whom was King Bimbisara.

The brothers practiced fire worship and worshiped Agni, the Brahmanic god of fire. In accordance with Brahmanic custom, they did not preach a religiously inspired way of living but instead simply performed religious rituals. It may have been because his teaching was radically different from that of the Kashyapa brothers that Shakyamuni sought to convert them to Buddhism, for if they, who were so eminent and respected, were to become awakened to the truth, their conversion might influence all the people of the kingdom of Magadha.

Early one evening, Shakyamuni called at the hermitage of Uruvilva-Kashyapa and begged to be permitted to stay the night. Uruvilva told Shakyamuni that all the rooms were occupied except the one in which the sacred fire was enshrined. When Shakyamuni said he wished to stay in that room, Uruvilva refused him, saying that a snake with magical powers lived in the room and therefore it would be dangerous to stay there. Shakyamuni insisted that he did not care what creature lived there, and at last Uruvilva reluctantly agreed to let him spend the night in that room.

At midnight, while Shakyamuni was sitting in meditation, a huge snake entered the room and spat fire; but Shakyamuni was in such a perfect state of spiritual concentration that flames poured forth from his whole body, and the snake could not approach him. It finally lost its magical powers and shrank so small that it could coil itself in an iron begging bowl placed near Shakyamuni.

Since Uruvilva and his disciples thought Shakyamuni would surely be killed by the huge venomous snake, they were astounded when they entered the room the next morning. They realized then that Shakyamuni possessed spiritual powers, and they paid respect to him; but they still looked down on him, believing him their inferior.

In India, there are still many ascetics who are possessed of mystical or paranormal faculties. They are capable of doing many things that defy logical explanation, such as curing disease, seeing what a person hundreds of kilometers away is doing and knowing what he is thinking, and even materializing before people far away. Explanations of such phenomena are still disputed among scientists, although most of them agree that there have been and still are ascetics who manifest paranormal abilities. With the progress of science, these phenomena will be explained one day.

Mystical or supernatural faculties seem to have been more highly developed among the ancients than among modern people. Great men of religion have been especially gifted in this respect; for example, the Bible records numerous miracles performed by Jesus. In ancient India, it was necessary for a person to have some sort of supernatural power in order to be considered a true sage. For Brahmanic priests of old those powers were more important than any other qualifications they might have had.

Buddhist scriptures record many incidents that demonstrate that Shakyamuni also possessed great supernatural powers; however, he did not think it necessary for a sage to have such powers. He held that a sage is a person who has reached that spiritual state of mind in which he is free of all illusion. Shakyamuni used his supernatural powers only when necessary and warned his disciples not to abuse their powers.

While other hermits and ascetics, adhering strictly to their principle of not teaching, simply conducted religious rites, offered prayers, and practiced divination, Shakyamuni preached to all people to awaken them to their illusions and to help them live in harmony with the Law of the universe. His teachings were beacons of true religion. However dramatically Uruvilva-Kashyapa might surpass others in supernatural powers and however learned he might be, in Shakyamuni's view he was not worthy to be called sage.

Uruvilva-Kashyapa, the leader of a noted religious community of five hundred disciples, behaved rather arrogantly toward Shakyamuni. Yet he thought that if this promising monk were to become his disciple his community might become more influential, and he urged Shakyamuni to stay longer at his hermitage. Shakyamuni, greatly desiring to convert Uruvilva to Buddhism, accepted the invitation.

Shakyamuni stayed with Uruvilva four days, and during that time he performed many wonders for Uruvilva's benefit. When Uruvilva became unsettled by the miracles, Shakyamuni said harshly, "You will never be a true *arhat* [honorable one], Uruvilva. Only a person who possesses great wisdom can rightly claim to be a true *arhat*."

With a new awareness, Uruvilva prostrated himself on the ground and, touching his forehead to Shakyamuni's feet, begged Shakyamuni's pardon, pleading: "Please make me your disciple." Shakyamuni counseled him gently: "Because you have five hundred disciples, you should not act on your own judgment alone. First consult with your disciples."

When Uruvilva talked with his disciples, they too recognized Shakyamuni's greatness, and they all wished to become his disciples. They showed their determination by throwing into the nearby Nairanjana River their altar and all the ceremonial implements used in worshiping the god of fire and by shaving their beards and matted hair. Shakyamuni gladly welcomed them into his Sangha.

Uruvilva-Kashyapa's two younger brothers, who lived on the lower reaches of the Nairanjana River, also were great ascetics; Nadi-Kashyapa had three hundred disciples, and Gaya-Kashyapa had two hundred. The two brothers were astonished to see an altar and the ceremonial implements used in worshiping their god floating down the river one day. Certain that something evil had befallen their elder brother, they rushed to his hermitage and found there a shaven-headed monk dressed in a brown robe. Looking about, they noticed many disciples shaven and clad in the same way as their brother.

They asked Uruvilva the meaning of what they saw, and he answered, "The way that we have sought is not the true path; I have now understood that clearly. To escape the sufferings of birth and death, there is nothing but the teachings of the Buddha. For this reason, I have become a follower of the Buddha with my disciples. You too should carefully consider your present state." Witnessing the conversion of their respected elder brother with their own eyes, the two younger brothers readily followed his advice. Thus in a very short space of time one thousand new disciples joined Shakyamuni.

With these new disciples Shakyamuni again started for Rajagriha. Along the way they stopped at Gayashirsha, a volcano from which could be seen the forest of Uruvilva, the Nairanjana River, and Mount Pragbodhi. Pointing to the plains and the mountains, Shakyamuni said to his disciples, "Monks! All things are burning. They are burning furiously. You must first know this. How do you interpret the words 'All things are burning'?

"The people's eyes are burning. When looking at things through their burning eyes, whatever they may see looks to them as if it were burning. Their ears are burning. When hearing things through their burning ears, whatever they may hear sounds to them as if it were burning. Their noses are burning. When smelling things through their burning noses, whatever they may smell has to them a burning odor. Their tongues are burning. When tasting things through their burning tongues, whatever they may eat tastes to them burned. Their bodies are burning. When feeling things through their burning bodies, whatever they may feel has to them a burning feeling. Their minds are burning. When thinking with their burning minds, whatever they may think seems to them to be burning.

"Monks! Do you know with what they are burning? They are burning with the flames of covetousness, anger, and ignorance. They are burning with the flames of birth, aging, illness, death, grief, suffering, distress, and agony.

"If you dislike these things, you can free yourselves from attachment to them. When you can do so, you can be liberated from the bonds of illusion and of suffering in this world."

This sermon later came to be called the Sermon on Burning and to occupy an important place in Buddhist thought. In this sermon Shakyamuni preached that sensations kindled by selfish instincts, covetousness, and attachment rooted in self-love cloud our vision and our minds and cause us all kinds of suffering. The enemy in humankind's heart that deceives and distresses us is likened to flames. Such expressions as the "flames of illusion" or the "flames of anger" found in later Buddhist teachings are based on this sermon and have become basic concepts in Buddhism.

A representative example of the subsequent use of the image of flames in teaching is found in "A Parable," chapter 3 of the Lotus Sutra. Here Shakyamuni employed the parable of a burning house to explain the condition of human society and the burning in our minds. As it is used in Buddhism, nirvana can indicate the state of tranquillity that enables us to extinguish both the fires in our minds and the raging flames enveloping society. The Sanskrit word *nirvana* means literally, "extinction," in the way that a candle is extinguished. Hence it would seem that the word nirvana can be used as the antithesis of the "flames of illusion."

The Sermon on Burning, with its fiery images, which Shakyamuni preached on the mountain Gayashirsha, was of far-reaching importance to Buddhism. At the same time, this sermon demonstrates his tactful means of teaching by adapting his words to suit the occasion and the audience. His listeners were men who, until just a few days earlier, had regarded fire as sacred and had followed a religion in which it was worshiped. They must have been astounded to hear Shakyamuni liken humankind's illusions to fire.

Their great shock, however, destroyed their superstitions and attachment to fire, which otherwise might have lingered in the depths of their minds even after they had become disciples of Shakyamuni. This manner of enlightening people, which we might think of as a type of shock treatment, is commonly called reverse enlightenment.

On most occasions, Shakyamuni seems to have favored direct enlightenment by gently drawing positive qualities out of the depths of people's minds. But with people whose illusions were like a deep-seated disease or with people who were excessively attached to their illusions, he sometimes used reverse enlightenment. He adapted his preaching method to the circumstances.

VULTURE PEAK AND THE BAMBOO GROVE MONASTERY Accompanied by his one thousand new disciples and the three Kashyapa brothers, Shakyamuni finally reached Rajagriha, where he was warmly welcomed by King Bimbisara. The king venerated Shakyamuni in various ways and tried to persuade Shakyamuni and his disciples to remain in his country by presenting them with a monastery in which to live.

King Bimbisara thought carefully. It would not be proper to build a monastery, a place for monks to live and to meditate on and practice the Law, near a noisy town. Yet if they were too far away, it would be inconvenient and would make it difficult for the monks to beg for alms. He then looked about for a fitting site and chose a bamboo grove located on the outskirts of Rajagriha, three or four hundred meters north of his palace. There he built the monastery. With great joy Shakyamuni accepted the monastery in the quiet grove. From that time on, Shakyamuni stayed there whenever he went to Rajagriha. The Bamboo Grove Monastery, the first Buddhist monastery, was one of two great Buddhist holy places for learning and practicing the Way: the other was the Jetavana Monastery built later at Shravasti, the capital of Kaushala, to the northwest.

Whenever he stayed at the Bamboo Grove Monastery, Shakyamuni would climb a mountain called Gridhrakuta, about five kilometers away, and preach his sermons there. A small hermitage was constructed on the mountain, and Shakyamuni would often stay there to meditate. The mountain is often mentioned in Buddhist literature; for example, the first chapter of the Lotus Sutra, "Introductory," begins with the words "Thus have I heard. Once the Buddha was staying at the City of Royal Palaces on Mount Gridhrakuta."

To make it easier for Shakyamuni to ascend the mountain, King Bimbisara laid out and paved a path from the foot of the mountain to the peak. This path, which has been restored, is called King Bimbisara's Road.

Gridhrakuta, which means Vulture Peak, received its name either because its summit resembled a vulture's head or because a flock of vultures lived there. Tradition says that it was atop Vulture Peak that Shakyamuni preached many key sutras, including the Lotus Sutra, the Sutra of Innumerable Meanings, and the Larger Amitabha Sutra. For Buddhists, it is certainly an important site among the sacred places in India.

Walking up King Bimbisara's Road and seeing the traces of the small hermitage and a speaker's platform at the top of Vulture Peak is a deeply moving experience: one almost expects to see the benevolent face of the Buddha.

While traveling by train in northern India, one seldom sees a mountain in the distance in the course of a journey of a day or two. The train passes through a seemingly endless plain, and in summer both the earth and the air seem parched. The monotony of traveling through that extraordinary, unchanging plain is finally broken when one arrives at present-day Rajgir, near the ruins of Rajagriha, and encounters a range of high mountains where the atmosphere is refreshing and the air is filled with the song of birds. Here one feels relief, and it is easy to understand Shakyamuni's fondness for Vulture Peak, where he so often preached.

The site of the ancient Bamboo Grove Monastery now looks like a park. The grove from which the monastery took its name has disappeared; only a small stand of bamboo imported from Japan by a Japanese botanist, a devout Buddhist, reminds one of the distant past. In time the bamboo should spread, and the grove should regain some of its former appearance.

THE CONVERSION OF
THREE GREAT DISCIPLES
Something momentous for Shakyamuni's community and for Buddhism occurred shortly after the Sangha took up residence in the Bamboo Grove

Monastery: three great men, Shariputra, Maudgalyayana, and Maha-Kashyapa, were converted to Buddhism.

Shariputra and Maudgalyayana, both sons of respected families from a village near Rajagriha, were reputed to have been brilliant since boyhood. Close friends, they became followers of Sanjaya, one of the six famous non-Buddhist teachers active in northern India at that time, and attained such an advanced state of spiritual development that Sanjaya entrusted his many disciples to them.

Although Sanjaya's teaching was excellent, Shariputra and Maudgalyayana could not truly free themselves of the bonds of illusion and suffering. Therefore Shariputra and Maudgalyayana set out to seek another teacher, promising to inform each other if either of them found a teacher who could show them the true path to freedom from the bonds of illusion and suffering.

In Rajagriha one day, Shariputra happened to notice a monk coming toward him. Though the monk was clad in a poor robe and had only an iron begging bowl, he looked serene and pure and carried himself with dignity. A single glance was enough to convince Shariputra that this monk was no ordinary person. He saluted the monk politely and asked, "Venerable monk! What sort of man are you? Under what teacher have you become a monk?"

The monk answered quietly, "I am called Ashvajit. My teacher is Shakyamuni, who is perfectly enlightened." Ashvajit was one of the five ascetics who became the first disciples of the Buddha when he rolled the wheel of the Law for the first time at Deer Park; and it was natural that Shariputra would have known nothing of him, since they met not many months after that first sermon.

Shariputra pressed Ashvajit for more information: "What is the teaching of your master?"

Ashvajit answered modestly, "It is only a short while since I became a disciple of Shakyamuni, so I do not know his teachings well. My teacher preaches to us that all things are produced by causation. The Tathagata has explained the causes and the way to eliminate them. This is the teaching of the World-honored One."

On hearing Ashvajit's words, Shariputra's heart leapt. He immediately realized that this was the very path he had sought so long, that it was indeed the teaching of freedom from the bonds of illusion and suffering. Elated, he asked Ashvajit, "Where does your teacher live?"

"He stays at the Bamboo Grove Monastery on the outskirts of Rajagriha."

"Thank you for your kindness, monk. I will go to your teacher together with my friend." Shariputra expressed his profound gratitude by prostrating himself before Ashvajit. He then went to Maudgalyayana, honoring the promise they had exchanged.

According to one story, when Maudgalyayana saw his friend Shariputra approaching, he at once thought that Shariputra had found the path to enlightenment. Listening to Shariputra, Maudgalyayana realized that he was right. The two soon decided to visit Shakyamuni.

Although not satisfied with his teacher's doctrine, Shariputra felt very grateful to his teacher, and he called on Sanjaya, saying, "Would you care to visit Shakyamuni with me and listen to his teaching?" Sanjaya declined, saying that out of consideration for his fame and position as a teacher, he could not after so long forsake his doctrine. Instead, he tried to dissuade Shariputra from meeting Shakyamuni. Shariputra abandoned the idea of Sanjaya's meeting Shakyamuni; but two hundred and fifty of Sanjaya's disciples, whose guidance had been entrusted to Shariputra, gladly followed him.

It is said that when Shakyamuni, who was preaching a sermon to a large group of people at the Bamboo Grove Monastery, saw Shariputra, Maudgalyayana, and Sanjaya's disciples approaching the monastery, he said, "Monks! Our friends Shariputra and Maudgalyayana come. These two will become my greatest disciples."

In "A Parable," chapter 3 of the Lotus Sutra, Shariputra says of the instruction he received from the Buddha:

> "Formerly I was attached to heretical views,
> Being a teacher of heretical mendicants.
> The World-honored One, knowing my heart,
> Uprooted my heresy and taught me nirvana."

Thus two extraordinary men joined Shakyamuni's community. Shariputra was later to become Shakyamuni's foremost disciple, respected for his outstanding wisdom, and Maudgalyayana was to be renowned for his great supernatural powers. The acceptance of these two men into Shakyamuni's community was indeed an important event in the history of Buddhism.

Another great disciple, who ranked with Shariputra and Maudgalyayana, was Maha-Kashyapa. In addition to the three Kashyapa brothers and a monk called Dashabala-Kashyapa, there was among Shakyamuni's disciples a fifth monk named Kashyapa. In order to distinguish him from the other disciples named Kashyapa, the title *maha* (literally, "great") was prefixed to his name, and he is known to us as Maha-Kashyapa. He is also called the Great Kashyapa in some sutra translations.

Maha-Kashyapa was born into a wealthy family that lived not far from Rajagriha. The family's financial power was comparable to that of the king; but his high social position and comfortable life notwithstanding,

Maha-Kashyapa had resolved in childhood to renounce the world. In ancient India, attaining spiritual freedom from the bonds of illusion and suffering seems to have been regarded as the supreme goal of human life. There were numerous instances of men born into rich families abandoning wealth and comfort to become monks. On the whole, the opposite trend is found today, when it is considered that people's greatest desires are fulfilled only by material comforts and riches.

In the case of Maha-Kashyapa's determination to renounce the world, his parents thought he would waver in his resolution to become a monk if he married, and they sought a suitable young woman. Because he could not openly defy his parents' wishes he had a skilled goldsmith fashion a life-size statue of a beautiful girl. Maha-Kashyapa then told his parents that he would marry the young woman who was as beautiful as the statue.

This condition imposed by Maha-Kashyapa sorely distressed his parents, but a Brahmanic priest of their acquaintance devised a solution for them. He had the statue mounted on a float and had it carried throughout the country with the announcement that all young women who worshiped the statue would have their wishes fulfilled. In this way the priest had the opportunity to view almost every young woman in the country. Fortunately or unfortunately, a beautiful young woman who looked just like the statue was at last discovered.

Kashyapa was obliged to marry the young woman, whose name was Bhadra; but possibly she had been predestined to become his wife. She was very religious and had a strong desire to seek after the Way. It is said that after they had been married for twelve years, they lived like brother and sister, achieving spiritual growth and encouraging one another.

One day, Bhadra ordered her servants to press oil from sesame seeds, but while drying and preparing the sesame seeds on mats spread in the garden, the servants found them infested with innumerable small insects.

They said to one another, "What cruelty to crush these insects together with the sesame seeds!"

"Do not worry about it. We have only to do as we are bidden by the mistress. We can but wonder if the greater fault lies with her."

Hearing their conversation, Bhadra ordered them to stop pressing oil from the seeds, and confining herself to her room, she thought deeply about the servants' words.

This story helps us understand why "oil expressing" is mentioned together with other grave sins in the following imprecation found in "Dharanis," chapter 26 of the Lotus Sutra:

> "May his doom be that of a parricide,
> His retribution that of an oil-expresser
> Or a deceiver with [false] measures and weights,
> Or of Devadatta who brought schism into the
> Sangha."

At the time of this incident Bhadra's husband, Maha-Kashyapa, was touring his fields and paused to watch his tenant farmers at their plowing. He noticed that countless worms were killed by the plows of the farmers as they turned up the earth. He thought, "Why must man carry off the lives of other living creatures so that he may live?" Unable to remain in the fields, he hurried back to his house.

When he arrived home, he found his wife, Bhadra, also in deep thought. They talked quietly for a time, and Maha-Kashyapa decided to become a monk and Bhadra a nun. Separately they set out on journeys to seek after the truth: Maha-Kashyapa to Rajagriha and Bhadra to Shravasti, the capital of Kaushala. It is said that when a community of Buddhist nuns was established with Shakyamuni's permission Bhadra joined it and was highly respected. Her name was introduced into some later Buddhist scriptures and was eventually translated into Chinese as "Wonderful and Wise."

Through his spiritual powers Shakyamuni had understood why Maha-Kashyapa was traveling toward Rajagriha and had taken the trouble to meet Maha-Kashyapa at a place midway between Rajagriha and Nalanda, where a great monastic Buddhist university would flourish many centuries later. From this action we know how great were Shakyamuni's hopes for Maha-Kashyapa.

As he passed before a *nyagrodha* tree standing by the road, Maha-Kashyapa saw sitting under the tree a man whose whole body emanated a golden light and who appeared to be an *arhat*. Maha-Kashyapa realized instinctively that this man was the very teacher he was seeking. At that moment, Shakyamuni spoke. "Kashyapa! I am glad you have come. Come, sit down here." Shakyamuni's address was without question a demonstration of his unique ability to instantly know the minds of others. From their first meeting there seems to have been a special, unspoken understanding between Shakyamuni and Maha-Kashyapa, which is illustrated in the following story.

Once when Shakyamuni was on Vulture Peak, Brahma, the great deity of the Hindu pantheon, visited a congregation of Buddhists there. He offered a yellow heavenly flower to the Buddha, prostrated himself, and reverently asked the Buddha to preach the Law. Sitting cross-legged, Shakyamuni held the flower out before all the Buddhists in the congregation without a word. There

was a hushed silence as the group waited for Shakyamuni to begin speaking. The people waited and waited,
but he remained silent. With the exception of Maha-
Kashyapa no one could comprehend what the Buddha
meant.

Then Shakyamuni's gaze sought Maha-Kashyapa.
When their eyes met, Maha-Kashyapa smiled broadly.
Nodding his head in satisfaction, Shakyamuni said, "I
possess the eye of the True Law, the marvelous mind of
nirvana, the true form of the formless, and the subtle
teachings of the Law, independent of words and transmitted beyond doctrine. This I have entrusted to Maha-
Kashyapa."

Shakyamuni's mute sermon was understood only by
Maha-Kashyapa, whose comprehension was perceived
by Shakyamuni. This famous story, which is recorded
in the Zen classic *Mumonkan* as Case 6, "The Buddha
Holds Out a Flower," has long been treasured by Zen
Buddhists because it illustrates the principle of understanding the Buddha's teaching directly through one's
own experience. Zen Buddhists, who value the attainment of one's own directly experienced understanding, revere Maha-Kashyapa as the first patriarch of Zen
Buddhism.

While Shakyamuni was alive, Maha-Kashyapa often
preached in his stead; and after the death of the Buddha,
Maha-Kashyapa presided over the First Council, at
which five hundred of the Buddha's leading disciples
met to compile all of the teachings of the Buddha. Maha-
Kashyapa was not only an outstanding disciple but also
a great leader.

It was Maha-Kashyapa who retold in verse the parable
of the poor son in "Faith Discernment," chapter 4 of the
Lotus Sutra. The character of the son in the parable in

many ways mirrors that of Maha-Kashyapa, who was content with the poverty of a mendicant. Maha-Kashyapa is said to have been foremost in the practice of the ascetic precepts known as *dhuta,* which required mendicants to live in a forest, to accept whatever seat might be offered, to live on alms, to use only one seat for both meditation and eating, to wear coarse garments, not to eat at unregulated times, to wear clothes made of discarded rags, to own only three robes, to live in or near a cemetery, to live under a tree, to live in the open air, and to sleep in a seated posture. Practice of the *dhutas* was intended to purify the body and the mind and to free the mendicant of all attachment to food, clothing, and dwelling place.

With the conversion of Shariputra, Maudgalyayana, and Maha-Kashyapa, who were to become the greatest of Shakyamuni's disciples, the stability of the Sangha was established. From about that time Shakyamuni's reputation began to increase and word of his teachings spread in all directions.

One can well imagine that with these disciples in his community the Buddha's sermons must have become more vivid and animated, since he so often directed his explanations of difficult truths to these disciples, who had a superior capacity to understand even his most advanced teachings. Certainly a great number of Shakyamuni's sermons recorded in the major sutras, such as the Lotus Sutra, are addressed directly to Shariputra and Maha-Kashyapa.

SHAKYAMUNI'S RETURN HOME   Rumor spread throughout northern India: Prince Siddhartha of the Shakyas, who had renounced the world, had at last attained unsurpassed enlightenment and become a buddha; and numbered among his followers were King Bimbisara of Magadha, some famous fire-worshiping Brahmans—the three Kashyapa brothers, who had been highly respected sages—Shariputra, Maudgalyayana, and Maha-Kashyapa.

When Shuddhodana, the king of the Shakyas and Shakyamuni's father, heard this rumor, he sent messengers inviting Shakyamuni to return to his homeland. On reaching Shakyamuni's community, the messengers were deeply moved by his magnificent, faultless character and by the aura of purity surrounding the people who were seeking after the truth under his guidance. Forgetting their mission, the messengers remained with Shakyamuni, becoming monks; none of them returned to the king's court.

Finally Shuddhodana sent his invitation with Udayin, who had been a close friend of Prince Siddhartha and who was now a young noble of great tact. The king was certain that, since he enjoyed life so much, Udayin would never become a monk. Yet on meeting Shakyamuni, Udayin too forgot his errand; being enlightened by the Buddha, he became a monk. When Udayin eventually recalled his mission, Shakyamuni decided it was time to visit his father and agreed to return to his homeland. At Shakyamuni's behest, Udayin went to Kapilavastu, the capital, to report Shakyamuni's decision to return home.

All Kapilavastu was astir with excitement over Udayin's news. Everyone believed that Prince Siddhartha would return home in triumph as the Buddha, and they thought what a great and respected person he must be. But when Shakyamuni and his disciples arrived in Kapilavastu, the people saw only a group of mendicants, all dressed alike in poor brown robes. Shakyamuni himself was clad as humbly as his disciples.

Shakyamuni and his companions declined the king's request to come to the palace and instead passed the night in the forest. The following day Shakyamuni and his disciples walked about the town begging for alms before going to the palace. Shuddhodana felt disgraced by Shakyamuni's shabby appearance and by his practice of begging; and the other nobles also were displeased with Shakyamuni for a time.

Quiet and composed, Shakyamuni entered the palace, undisturbed by the feelings of the king and the many members of the family. Shakyamuni told Shuddhodana that he had brought an unsurpassingly great gift, the immortal, true Law. King Shuddhodana, who had looked on Shakyamuni as merely his son, came to understand Shakyamuni's teaching and to realize that his son was now the Buddha, the Teacher of Gods and Men. From that time on, the king treated Shakyamuni with respect and addressed him in the formal speech reserved for addressing superiors.

Viewed superficially, Shakyamuni's abandoning his father in his renunciation of the world seems unfilial; but from the standpoint of humankind's eternal life, blood relationships in this world are only temporary, transitory bonds between human beings. The question is whether humankind sets greater value on its fleeting existence or on its eternal life. A Buddhist proverb says that if a man becomes a monk, nine generations of his family will be reborn in heaven. Since Shakyamuni became the Buddha in order to save all sentient beings from their sufferings, how very much more should his renunciation of the world have benefited his father's eternal life.

Several years after Shakyamuni's first visit to his homeland, Shuddhodana became bedridden because of old age. The king, who was, it is said, ninety-seven years old and knew that his life was nearing its end, again desired to see his son, as well as his grandson and nephews who had become Shakyamuni's disciples. Shakyamuni was staying on Vulture Peak at the time; but when he received word of his father's condition, he quickly returned home, accompanied by his son, Rahula; his cousin Ananda; his younger half brother, Nanda; and other disciples.

King Shuddhodana was gladdened to see Shakyamuni and asked him to place his hands on his father's body and preach a final sermon for the dying king.

Shakyamuni said to Shuddhodana, "There is nothing to fear, father. Your virtue is most pure and your mind is undefiled by evil. Remember the Law that you have heard until now and put your mind at ease and at peace."

Taking Shakyamuni's hand in his, the old king pressed it to his heart and then expired, as if sleeping, with a serene expression on his face.

Shakyamuni himself, aided by Rahula, Ananda, and Nanda, carried the litter bearing Shuddhodana's corpse to the funeral pyre; and afterward they buried the king's ashes and bones. Many nobles who had sympathized with the old king in his disgrace and loneliness and who had secretly condemned Shakyamuni for his lack of filial devotion for the first time understood that the king actually had been very fortunate indeed.

It has been said that King Shuddhodana was reborn in the highest of the four meditation heavens in the Realm of Form, in which beings have no bodies and experience only the sensations of pleasure and freedom from pain, which may prove the worth of the proverb about the family of a man who becomes a monk. I think we should give that proverb more consideration. As I said earlier, we need not actually become monks these days, but we must attach importance to becoming monks spiritually. If we do, we shall influence those around us and unconsciously we shall benefit them. In this sense, the old proverb still has meaning for us today.

THE CONVERSION OF
SHAKYAMUNI'S FAMILY

When Shakyamuni arrived at the palace in Kapilavastu on his first visit home after his attainment of buddhahood, he found his whole clan assembled there. Only Princess Yashodhara, the wife of Prince Siddhartha, stayed away: she did not wish to meet the former prince in public. She remained in her room in the palace and thought that if Shakyamuni loved her as much as he had when he was still Prince Siddhartha he would surely come to her.

Yashodhara had abandoned herself to grief and despair when her husband left her and their child to become a monk, but she soon recovered and devoted herself to rearing her son, Rahula. She did, however, cease wearing makeup after the prince left the palace, and on being told that he wore a brown robe, she herself wore one of the same color. Hearing that he ate but one meal a day and that he slept under a tree or on a stone, she followed his example. Thus, at least in her mind, she still shared the prince's life. Because of her deep feeling for her husband, regardless of however honored he might have become as the Buddha, many emotions must have stirred within her when she learned of Shakyamuni's homecoming.

Shakyamuni, who understood the princess's feelings,

went to her room accompanied by only two disciples, Shariputra and Maudgalyayana. When she saw Shakyamuni, she was so overcome that she could not utter a word: she could only weep at his feet. Shakyamuni stood quietly while she wept. Before long she regained her senses and realized that her husband had really never belonged to her but had always been meant to become the Buddha and to save all beings from their sufferings. Wiping the tears from her eyes, she stood and bowed serenely to him.

He looked on her loveliness with affection and nodded his head in satisfaction. He then spoke to her of her life in a previous existence: "You have been able to hear the Righteous Law through the special providence of the Buddha. This is due to the good karma that you produced by good deeds in your previous existence. After today forget your sorrow of the past and lead a happy and grateful life."

On the morning of the seventh day following this meeting Shakyamuni, together with his disciples, was begging food in the town, as usual. Princess Yashodhara made her young son, Rahula, dress formally and then permitted him to see his father for the first time. The princess said to her son, "Rahula, look at the monks over there. Among them you can see a great monk who has remarkable dignity. That man is your father."

With a doubting look, Rahula said to his mother, "I never knew that I had a father. My grandfather, the old king, is the only man who has been a father to me."

Yashodhara replied, "Well may you say so; yet that very great monk is your father. Go and see him and ask him to give you his property. He possesses an immensely valuable treasure that no one has yet seen."

Eventually Shakyamuni entered the palace to receive

food. Rahula went to Shakyamuni and said innocently, "Father! I am very happy to be at your side." The boy beamed with joy all during his father's meal. When Shakyamuni rose from his seat to return to the forest, Rahula ran after him, saying, "Father! Please give your treasure to me." No one prevented his following Shakyamuni, and as Princess Yashodhara watched her son leave, tears streamed down her cheeks. Rahula, remaining in the forest with his father, became a monk and was given the greatest treasure in life.

After Rahula joined his father, Princess Yashodhara became a recluse and led a solitary existence in the inner part of the palace. Some years after King Shuddhodana had died and Shakyamuni's foster mother, Mahaprajapati, had become a nun (she was the first female member of the Buddhist community), Princess Yashodhara resolved to become a nun and set out for Vaishali, the capital of the nation of the Vrijis, where Mahaprajapati lived. Refusing the comfort of a carriage that was offered to her, she journeyed on foot with her serving women. On finally reaching Vaishali, she immediately joined the Buddhist community of nuns.

In the India of that time, women were not permitted to become members of religious communities. When Mahaprajapati sought Shakyamuni's permission to enter the Sangha, he refused her request three times. His refusal seems to have stemmed not from a discriminatory attitude toward women but from an anxiety to maintain discipline in the Buddhist community. However, because Shakyamuni had vowed to save *all* sentient beings from their sufferings, he relented and permitted women to become nuns, thus breaking with the accepted practice of that time. His was unquestionably a revolutionary decision.

Both Mahaprajapati and Yashodhara became outstanding nuns: they paved the way for female Buddhists in later ages and set an example for all Buddhist nuns. The merits of the two nuns' piety and religious practices are said to have been the greatest among the female mendicants.

Later, as a nun, Yashodhara went from Vaishali to the Jetavana Monastery, where Shakyamuni lived, and studied there under him. She soon attained great serenity and happily led a religious life. Since Rahula, who was also a member of the Sangha, lived at the Jetavana Monastery, Yashodhara made her home close by. She went often to receive instruction from Shakyamuni, and with his permission, she sometimes called on Rahula.

Yashodhara was loved and respected by lay Buddhists, monks, and nuns alike because of her gentle personality. It is said that the believers in the nearby town of Shravasti were so earnest in giving her alms that she was able to live in more comfort than she had at court. Yashodhara did not enjoy such ease, however, and she moved to Vaishali in the hope of living a life of genuine mendicancy. Finding there the same situation as at Shravasti, she again moved, this time to the vicinity of Rajagriha. There at last she was able to lead the simple life of a dedicated Buddhist nun.

THE CONVERSION OF THE SHAKYAS   Shakyamuni's first visit to Kapilavastu after attaining buddhahood had far-reaching effects both in and around the capital. The most striking occurrence was the conversion of a great many of the members of Shakyamuni's clan. Among the Shakyas mentioned by name in the Lotus Sutra are Nanda, Aniruddha, Ananda, Devadatta, and Upali.

Nanda, the son of King Shuddhodana and his second wife, Mahaprajapati, Shakyamuni's foster mother, was Shakyamuni's younger half brother.

Aniruddha was a cousin of Shakyamuni. It is said that he once dozed off while listening to Shakyamuni preach, and the Buddha admonished him for his sloth. He was so inspired by the Buddha's rebuke he vowed that he would never sleep again. He eventually lost his eyesight, but he acquired a "supernatural eye," capable of seeing everything.

Ananda, another cousin of Shakyamuni, attended the Buddha until the Buddha's death, thus having the opportunity to hear him preach every day. Ananda, who was famous for his excellent memory, is supposed to have memorized all the Buddha's sermons and to have recited them at the First Council. He is also said to have been the person who recalled the many episodes that bring variety and realism to the life stories of the Buddha and his disciples.

Devadatta, Ananda's elder brother, was at first a follower of the Buddha, but he later turned against Shakyamuni and his community. Because of its importance, I shall discuss the story of Devadatta's betrayal more fully below.

In contrast to these relatives of Shakyamuni, who all came from noble families, Upali, a simple barber in Kapilavastu, was a member of the lowest social caste. He wondered why so many men had come to him to have their heads shaved after Shakyamuni's return to his homeland. Upali asked about it and learned that many people, attracted by Shakyamuni's great virtue and peerless teachings, were becoming monks, disciples of the Buddha.

Upali also learned that anyone could become a member of Shakyamuni's community, without regard for birth, lineage, or station, and that all members would be treated equally. Upali, a former slave, then entered the Sangha of the Buddha with an untroubled mind. Assiduous in his observance of the Buddhist precepts, Upali was later reputed to have been the disciple with the most comprehensive knowledge of the precepts of Shakyamuni's community.

It is interesting to note that, with the exception of Devadatta, all these early Shakya converts were to be numbered among the ten greatest disciples of the Buddha.

DEVADATTA'S TREACHERY   Devadatta seems to have been an admirable and able person throughout much of his life. In his youth he was a serious rival of Prince Siddhartha in both learning and sports, though he always remained a hairbreadth behind the prince. He was very self-important by nature but at the same time appears to have suffered feelings of inferiority, which seem to have provoked his later rebellion against Shakyamuni.

On the way back to Rajagriha after his first visit to Kapilavastu, Shakyamuni stopped in a forest, where he preached the Law to his new disciples. Most of them immediately acquired the enlightenment of an *arhat;* but it was not until three months after the Buddha's death that Ananda was finally able to free himself of all illusions and cravings and become an *arhat,* and Devadatta never became an *arhat.* Ananda's impulsive nature prevented his attaining the enlightenment of an *arhat*, and Devadatta's arrogance hindered him.

After this sermon in the forest Devadatta zealously studied Buddhist doctrine under Shakyamuni. He memorized all the teachings that he heard and would reconfirm what he had heard whenever something seemed unclear or he had questions; and he also endeavored to practice seated meditation. To his regret, however, he was not able to alter his self-centered nature.

Devadatta observed that Shakyamuni's community of several thousand monks had prospered and was generously endowed by kings and wealthy believers. Despite the fact that he studied and practiced the Buddha's teachings in order to improve his character, he could not control his burning ambition to lead Shakyamuni's community and to satisfy his sense of self-importance by standing at the head of such a large number of monks. Because he could not attain the level of spiritual development of the Buddha's other leading disciples, Devadatta daily experienced irritation and the feeling of being ignored by his fellow monks. Devadatta is said to have passed some thirty years nursing such feelings.

One account says that the motive for the actions that led to Devadatta's downfall was his strong desire to acquire supernatural powers. He could barely restrain his envy of the monks who were possessed of such powers and even asked Shakyamuni to teach him how to acquire such abilities. Shakyamuni spoke with Devadatta about this desire: "Those who have attained enlightenment possess supernatural powers as a matter of course. You are mistaken to seek the power itself. You must first perceive the universal truth and free yourself from all illusions and attachments to this world."

But Devadatta, unable to reconcile himself to pursuing that method of acquiring supernatural powers, called on various monks who had such powers. Although most monks refused his request, Dashabala-Kashyapa, who was renowned for his powers, consented willingly; and Devadatta attained numerous supernatural powers, although he later lost them. It was at about the time that he acquired these powers that his long-suppressed jealousy began to surface. His conceit grew and he was no longer awed by Shakyamuni or by Shariputra and Maudgalyayana.

Devadatta went to Rajagriha and succeeded in ingratiating himself with Prince Ajatashatru, the son of King Bimbisara, and in making the prince his patron. He then plotted to destroy the close relations between King Bimbisara and the devoted community of Shakyamuni's followers, and together with the prince to establish a new religious community of his own followers. He instigated a plot for the prince to murder the king and thus gain the throne.

Following Devadatta's plan, the young prince Ajatashatru imprisoned his father and began starving the old king to death. Then when the prince learned that his mother, Queen Vaidehi, had painted her body with honey and flour in order to smuggle sustenance to the king when she visited him, Ajatashatru shut her up in the inner part of the palace. I might mention here that it was for Queen Vaidehi, who had asked him for spiritual salvation, that Shakyamuni went to the palace in Rajagriha and preached the Sutra of Meditation on Amitabha Buddha, one of the three scriptures of the Pure Land sect of Japanese Buddhism.

Around the time of King Bimbisara's imprisonment Devadatta proposed to Shakyamuni the so-called Five

Practices, a stringent set of new precepts for the Sangha:

1. Do not allow monks to enter villages; permit them to live only in remote forests throughout their lives.

2. Do not allow monks to accept invitations from lay believers; permit them to live only as beggars throughout their lives.

3. Do not allow monks to accept robes offered by lay believers; permit them to wear only tattered robes made of rags throughout their lives.

4. Do not allow monks to enter houses with roofs; permit them to live only under trees throughout their lives.

5. Do not permit monks to eat the flesh of animals or fish throughout their lives and punish those who violate this rule.

These extreme precepts put forth by Devadatta were contrary to the doctrine of the Middle Path—the path between the extremes of self-mortification and self-indulgence—that Shakyamuni preached. Shakyamuni believed that the monks' practices should aim at freeing them of illusions and attachments, and he felt that forcing them to concentrate so much on the unimportant concerns of food, clothing, and shelter would be counterproductive. Although there are some people who can attain enlightenment through such rigorous ascetic practices, they are in the minority. True salvation is rooted in the human capacity to be saved regardless of individual circumstances—this is what Shakyamuni believed.

The overly strict regulation of such nonessential matters as food, clothing, and shelter does not contribute to the saving of sentient beings from their sufferings. If unvarying, inflexible rules are forced on people without regard for differences in climate, race, customs, individual constitution, and character, people become so preoccupied with such regulations that they are apt to overlook the essential purpose of their practice, which is to rid themselves of illusions. For that reason Shakyamuni had not established precepts for his community of believers. It was enough for his disciples to vow their devotion to the Three Treasures.

However, as Shakyamuni's community grew and various kinds of people entered it, the words and conduct of some of his disciples disturbed its harmony. Whenever that happened Shakyamuni admonished the offenders and taught them how to live correctly; this was the origin of the Buddhist precepts. The rules containing the provisions of the precepts, the reasons for instituting the precepts, the punishment for violations of the precepts, and the way to maintain the precepts, were called the Buddhist regulations.

But all Shakyamuni's rules for Buddhists were based on the truth of the Middle Path. Therefore, when Devadatta pressed Shakyamuni to adopt stricter rules of asceticism for the Sangha, Shakyamuni refused flatly. Some say that it was this refusal that finally prompted Devadatta to act against Shakyamuni. Declaring publicly that Shakyamuni had lived a life of luxury, Devadatta began to rebel openly against Shakyamuni.

Devadatta made several attempts to kill Shakyamuni: he sent thirty-one expert archers against the Buddha; he dropped a boulder off a cliff onto the Buddha when he was passing by below; he fed wine to a rogue elephant and then set the maddened beast on Shakyamuni when he was begging for alms. All these base efforts ended in failure, although one of them did have serious consequences.

A splinter of the boulder dropped by Devadatta cut Shakyamuni's foot badly, causing it to bleed profusely, and he returned to the monastery in great pain. Aroused by Devadatta's outrage, Shakyamuni's disciples shouted that they could no longer forgive the man. Warning them that they must never descend to violence, Shakyamuni quietly lay down on his bed. Because Shakyamuni's wound did not appear to be healing properly, Jivaka, a famous physician of Rajagriha, was called to treat Shakyamuni's foot.

Having mentioned Jivaka, I should like to point out here that Shakyamuni's views were by no means otherworldly; he believed, for example, that complaints that could be remedied through science should be referred to scientists. Though Jivaka was King Bimbisara's private physician, when he became a devout believer in Buddhism he treated the ailments of Shakyamuni and his disciples. Shakyamuni urged Jivaka to accept common people as patients, too, and directed him to live outside the palace. The remains of Jivaka's residence can still be seen on the way from present-day Rajgir to Vulture Peak.

Eventually King Ajatashatru, Devadatta's patron, realized the enormity of his offenses and, repenting in Shakyamuni's presence, became a follower of the Buddha's teachings. Devadatta fell into a piteous state, and in despair he repeated many of his evil deeds, with no hope of a happier existence.

Looking at Devadatta's life, we can understand that he was not simply an evil man but, instead, a worldly man. If he had not strayed from the path of the Buddha's teachings, he could have lived a fruitful life; but because he could not control his sense of self-importance, he reduced himself to a state of utter wretchedness. Since his character, emotions, and conduct all reveal weaknesses still common among people today, we should not dismiss him as just an evil person intrinsically different from us.

There is a surprising chapter in the Lotus Sutra in which Shakyamuni assures even Devadatta of enlightenment. In chapter 12, "Devadatta," Shakyamuni says, "The attainment of Perfect Enlightenment, and the widespread saving of the living—all this is due to the good friendship of Devadatta."

This chapter of the Lotus Sutra teaches the theory of the attainment of buddhahood even by evil people. At the same time, it is also noteworthy because it demonstrates Shakyamuni's tolerance and his condemnation of the offense but not the offender. The ability of evil people to attain buddhahood is based on the theory that all human beings are essentially equal and of one nature. Evil has no existence on its own: it is the product of an evil cause and an evil effect. Thus, when the evil cause and the evil effect disappear, evil is extinguished.

Shakyamuni declared "All this is due to the good friendship of Devadatta," for two reasons. First, through Devadatta's betrayal of the Law, the correctness of Shakyamuni's teaching of the Middle Path became still more apparent, and Shakyamuni's whole community was enabled to follow a right course and avoid being misled to a wrong path. Second, because Devadatta revealed his failings as a man and exhibited the worst side of human nature Shakyamuni himself learned something and his enlightenment deepened. Shakyamuni's words "All this is due to the good friendship of Devadatta" reflect a profound teaching of Buddhism: Be thankful for all things.

IN SHRAVASTI Sudatta, a rich merchant who lived in Shravasti, the capital of Kaushala, far to the northwest of Rajagriha, went to Rajagriha on business shortly after Shakyamuni first arrived there. Whenever Sudatta visited Rajagriha he stayed at the home of his wealthy brother-in-law. One evening when he chanced to go there, he found his younger sister's whole family busying themselves about something and paying no attention to him although he was usually welcomed warmly. When he asked a maidservant who the master's guests might be, she replied that the Buddha and his disciples were soon to visit the residence.

The instant he heard the name, Sudatta, who had been blessed with a generous and compassionate nature, yearned to meet the Buddha. Thus he went to the Bamboo Grove Monastery, where he was fortunate enough to hear the Buddha preach.

Sudatta at once devoted himself to the Buddha and his teachings and begged Shakyamuni to allow him to build a monastery in Shravasti for the Buddha and his disciples. Shakyamuni gave his permission, and soon after Sudatta returned to Shravasti he found a suitable site for the monastery he eventually built. I have already explained how he obtained the land (see page 16).

Because Sudatta gave food and shelter to orphans, lonely old people, and the needy, he was called Anathapindada, "one who gives to the needy." The monastery that Sudatta built was called the Jetavana-Anathapindada Monastery because the land it stood on was originally owned by Prince Jeta and later purchased by Anathapindada, but it came to be called simply the Jetavana Monastery. Shakyamuni often stayed at the Jetavana Monastery, and he preached many sermons there.

At about the time of the founding of the Jetavana Monastery, Queen Mallika of Kaushala became a follower of the Buddha, and under her influence King Prasenajit also became a devout believer. The king asked

Shakyamuni for advice on everything from the problems of life to government policies. It is said that he once visited the Jetavana Monastery three times on the same day to see the Buddha.

In Shravasti there lived a female lay believer known to us as Mrigara-matri, who donated the land for the Mrigara-matri Hall, which is mentioned in various sutras. This woman, who was married to a rich man, Mrigara of Shravasti, did much together with Sudatta to support the Sangha of the Buddha. Thus, as we see, Buddhism flourished both at Shravasti and at Rajagriha.

Other places in northern India are also remembered in connection with the Buddha's teaching mission. Among them, Vaishali, the capital of the country of the Vriji tribes, is especially important. Shakyamuni often visited the Great Forest Monastery on the outskirts of Vaishali and preached the Law there. The Sutra of Meditation on the Bodhisattva Universal Virtue, the closing sutra of the Threefold Lotus Sutra, was preached there by the Buddha.

4 · The Great Decease

WHY PREACH THE Shakyamuni spent the years be-
LOTUS SUTRA tween his enlightenment and his
death at the age of eighty carrying
his message to the people of north central India. It is
said that, since he was always barefoot, the soles of his
feet became leather-hard during those years of wandering from town to town and village to village.

While Jesus is believed to have devoted three years to
his teaching mission, Shakyamuni's teaching ministry
spanned forty-five years, and his sermons are said to
have numbered some eighty-four thousand. Although
the contents of the sermons themselves were committed
to memory by his disciples (and much later written
down), no complete account of his life was ever compiled
by those who knew him (the few reliable biographies we
have were written long after his death).

By carefully studying extant sutras, however, we can
trace the general course of Shakyamuni's life during the
period beginning a few months after his first rolling of

the Law-wheel at Deer Park and including his ministry in and around Rajagriha, as well as during the last few months preceding his death. But it is impossible for scholars today to establish an accurate chronological record of his life, either prior to his enlightenment or during the forty-five years he spent wandering throughout north central India.

From the mentions of particular places and people and from the passing references to historical events that we find in various sutras, we are able to infer that, for example, a certain sutra must have been preached before King Bimbisara was murdered by Prince Ajatashatru or that another sutra must have been preached after King Prasenajit had become a follower of Shakyamuni. However, we cannot possibly determine the correct chronology of most of the Buddha's sermons, which do not contain such references.

Chih-i (538–97), the great patriarch of the T'ien-t'ai sect of Chinese Buddhism, made an exhaustive study of the Buddhist scriptures available to him; and by grouping sutras together on the basis of their content, he established a rough chronology for the Buddha's sermons. Chih-i arranged the sutras within the following periods: (1) the Flower Garland Sutra period, during which that sutra was expounded; (2) the Agama sutras period, during which those sutras, which comprise the Theravada canon, were expounded; (3) the Mahayana sutras period, during which the majority of the scriptures comprising the Mahayana canon were expounded; (4) the Perfect Wisdom sutras period, during which those sutras were expounded; and (5) the Lotus Sutra and Sutra of the Great Decease period, during which those two sutras were expounded.

Later Buddhist scholars, amplifying Chih-i's work, developed a more exacting chronology that incorporated time spans for each of the periods specified by Chih-i. According to those scholars: (1) the lengthy Flower Garland Sutra was expounded during the first twenty-one days following the Buddha's enlightenment (it is now believed, however, that Shakyamuni himself did not actually preach this sutra, which sets forth basic Mahayana tenets, but that it is the creation of compilers who drew on late sermons to compose it); (2) the Agama sutras were expounded during the following twelve years; (3) the Mahayana sutras were expounded during the following eight years; (4) the Perfect Wisdom sutras were expounded during the following twenty-two years; and (5) the Lotus Sutra was expounded during the following eight years, with the Sutra of the Great Decease being expounded during the day and night preceding the death of the Buddha.

According to this chronology, Shakyamuni's teaching ministry spanned fifty years, but subsequent research has established that he actually taught only forty-five years. Although we cannot rely on the time spans in the chronology given above, we can be fairly confident that Shakyamuni preached his sermons in roughly the order suggested by Chih-i.

It is impossible to say which of Shakyamuni's sermons are more important and which are less so. The truth of his early teachings is no less perfect than that of his later teachings. Shakyamuni expounded his teachings in accordance with the needs and abilities of each listener. Sometimes he preached an easily understood, practical doctrine of life, and at other times he preached a profound philosophy. But in reviewing all the sermons preached during his lifetime, we can see that the truth he preached was consistent and unchanging from his first sermon to his last.

For instance, in his first rolling of the Law-wheel, Shakyamuni expounded to the five ascetics the doctrine of the Four Noble Truths, that is, the truths of suffering, the cause of suffering, and the path by which suffering can be extinguished. During the final journey before his death he preached the same doctrine to the courtesan Amrapali. It is said that Amrapali, becoming a devout follower of Shakyamuni, released all the harlots in her employ and eventually became a nun.

There must have been a difference between Shakyamuni's method of preaching to the five ascetics, with their great learning and experience, and his method of preaching to a rich and beautiful courtesan. Yet, the doctrine that he preached (the Four Noble Truths) was itself unchanged. The result of Shakyamuni's teaching—the enlightenment and salvation of the listener—was always the same, regardless of what teaching method he used. As is seen in the Buddhist scriptures, all the Buddha's sermons dealt with the Law, combining right reasoning with right expression to convey the teaching that, in Shakyamuni's own words, is "good at its commencement, good in its middle, and good at the end."

In "Preaching," chapter 2 of the Sutra of Innumerable Meanings, which the Buddha delivered immediately before expounding the Lotus Sutra, Shakyamuni gives his reasons for preaching the Lotus Sutra toward the end of his long ministry:

"Good sons! After six years' right sitting under the Bodhi tree of the wisdom throne, I could accomplish Perfect Enlightenment. With the Buddha's eye I saw all the laws and understood that they were inexpressible. Wherefore? I knew that the natures and desires of all living beings were not equal. As their natures and desires were not equal, I preached the Law variously. It was with tactful power that I preached the Law variously. In forty years and more, the truth has not been revealed yet. Therefore living beings' powers of attainment are too different to accomplish supreme buddhahood quickly."

By this time the disciples who had practiced at Shakyamuni's side for some forty-odd years had attained advanced levels of spiritual growth and Shakyamuni himself had become aware of his approaching death. Thus he determined: "I must now preach the final, profound truth." As an introduction he expounded the Sutra of Innumerable Meanings, and after meditating for some time, he finally began to preach the Lotus Sutra.

What is the final, profound truth? In brief, it is the finding of the infinite life of humankind within the eternal life-force of the universe.

The true nature of humankind, in its union with the eternal life-force of the universe, is called the buddha-nature. The Lotus Sutra teaches that all beings possess the buddha-nature (or potential for enlightenment) equally, that we should respect this potential in one another and encourage one another to develop and fulfill this potential, and that the noblest form of Buddhist practice is the way of the bodhisattva, who devotes himself to attaining enlightenment not only for himself but for all sentient beings.

When Shakyamuni had finished expounding the Lotus Sutra and its closing sutra, he may have decided to meet death in his childhood home, Kapilavastu, for the final journey on which he embarked was carrying him in that general direction.

SHAKYAMUNI'S SPIRITUAL POWERS   Accompanied by Ananda and a number of other disciples, Shakyamuni began to make his way north from the vicinity of Rajagriha. Shakyamuni, who was then eighty years old, suffered constantly from the severe back pain with which he had been afflicted for several years. Buddhist scriptures record the Buddha's comment at that time: "Ananda, I am old and frail. I am eighty. Like an old cart that can be kept in operation only with the help of leather thongs, the body of the Tathagata can be kept going only with much help."

One must bow before the great spiritual powers that enabled Shakyamuni to continue his mission at such an advanced age and in the face of the many hardships he experienced during his final journey.

I have already mentioned how, on his way into Vaishali from Pataliputra (present-day Patna), Shakyamuni converted the courtesan Amrapali. An often-told story says that around that time Shakyamuni declined to receive a group of Vriji aristocrats because he had accepted an invitation to dine at the home of Amrapali and did not wish to be late. It is obvious that in Shakyamuni's mind all human beings, whether noble or courtesan, are possessed of the buddha-nature. It is related that even though the nobles were not able to see Shakyamuni, they learned much from his refusal and returned to their homes deeply impressed.

The rainy season set in at about the time Shakyamuni was staying in Vaishali. The rainy season, brought to

India by the monsoons, lasts roughly from June to October, and it rains almost constantly during this period. As a result of the rains, in many parts of the country the rivers flood and people have great difficulty getting about. Even today infectious diseases sometimes plague rural districts when the filthy flood waters contaminate wells.

India's rainy season still creates problems today, but twenty-five hundred years ago it was virtually impossible to travel in the rural districts during those months. Hence, during the rainy season Shakyamuni and his disciples stayed at a monastery for spiritual training centered on meditation. This system of training was known as *varshika*, or "training during the rainy season."

Shakyamuni began the final *varshika* before his death at the Great Forest Monastery outside Vaishali, but because the town was suffering a severe food shortage he instructed his disciples to disperse to nearby areas while he remained behind with Ananda.

The intense heat, humidity, and damp of the rainy season could not have been good for Shakyamuni's failing health, and in addition he fell seriously ill after having eaten horse fodder because of the scarcity of other food. The severity of his illness, coupled with yet another attack of the back ailment that had long troubled him, brought him very close to death. Yet he thought, "It is not proper for me to die now. I must see my disciples once more and give them my final instruction. I must overcome this disease by being right minded and live a while longer."

Through his unsurpassed spiritual powers, great effort, and mindfulness, Shakyamuni did overcome his illness and prolong his life for a while. It was with great relief that Ananda said to Shakyamuni, "When I saw that you were seriously ill I felt as if everything were going dark before my eyes. But I took some small comfort from the thought that you would not leave the world without parting from the monks."

Shakyamuni answered solemnly, "Ananda, I have taught them everything. I have no pronouncements for the Sangha. Ananda, you must all be lamps unto yourselves. You must rely on yourselves and no one else. You must make the Law your light and support, and rely on nothing else."

This address is remembered in Buddhism as the teaching of "Make the self your light, make the Law your light." "Make the self your light" refers not to the self that is filled with illusions but to the self that lives in the Law. "Make the Law your light" means that one must burn with the fire of the Law and cast its light over society. Shakyamuni's closing exhortation means that one must rely on that universal truth alone, ignoring all else. The teaching of "Make the self your light, make the Law your light" is still valid today.

THE DECEASE   Sensing that his death was near, Shakyamuni summoned the disciples he had earlier sent away, and together they continued the journey to the northwest. Though his back frequently caused him severe pain, Shakyamuni persisted in the arduous trek. Whenever he was approached by a person seeking his teachings, he stopped and preached earnestly. Eventually Shakyamuni and his disciples reached the village of Pava, not far from Kushinagara (the capital of the kingdom of Malla), and stayed a while at a grove there.

The grove was owned by Chunda, a devout Buddhist layman, who felt deeply honored by the Buddha's presence and went to listen to him preach. Rejoicing in his encounter with the Buddha, Chunda asked permission to serve him a meal on the following day. Shakyamuni gladly agreed, but after eating the meal prepared by Chunda, the Buddha's condition suddenly worsened drastically.

Shocked by Shakyamuni's sudden decline and filled with great sorrow, Ananda thought, "In the dish served by Chunda, I found certain mushrooms that are considered special delicacies. Surely the World-honored One must have been poisoned by them."

Observing the sudden deterioration of Shakyamuni's illness and assuming that it was caused by the meal he had served, Chunda was heartbroken and suffered intense remorse.

Shakyamuni, noticing Chunda's distress, called Ananda to his side to ask what had happened. Ananda replied, "World-honored One! Chunda has erred irreparably in serving that meal to you. He offered you food so poisonous as to shorten your life."

Despite his acute pain Shakyamuni reproved Ananda gently: "Ananda! Chunda need feel no remorse because the meal he served to me has hastened my death. I was given a bowl of rice gruel by Sujata, a village girl, just before I attained enlightenment. The merit of the meal that I have accepted from Chunda, immediately before my death, is equal to that of the rice gruel offered by Sujata. Tell Chunda I say this and ease his mind." When he repeated Shakyamuni's compassionate, comforting words to Chunda, Ananda shared with Chunda an overwhelming gratitude to the Buddha.

Aware that his death was close at hand, Shakyamuni decided to die in Kushinagara; thus he left Pava in spite of the gravity of his illness. One account says that, although Pava lay only a few kilometers from Kushinagara, Shakyamuni stopped twenty-five times along the way to rest, which indicates how difficult the journey was for him. But whenever tribesmen of the Malla kingdom asked him to preach, he ignored his pain and willingly delivered sermons to them, restraining Ananda, who was worried about his illness.

When Shakyamuni and his disciples finally reached Kushinagara, they entered the *shala* grove on the edge of town. Shakyamuni asked that a bed be made for him between two twin-trunked *shala* trees, directing Ananda to place the head of the bed to the north.

In tears, Ananda did as he was instructed, and Shakyamuni lay on his right side in a comfortable position, with his legs drawn up. It is recorded that at that moment the *shala* trees burst into bloom out of season, shedding a rain of flowers on his body, and that divine music and voices filled the air in homage to the World-honored One.

At about this time, Subhadra, an aged wandering ascetic who had lived near Kushinagara and had heard the rumor that Shakyamuni would pass away at midnight, came to the grove asking that the Buddha teach him the true Law. Believing that Shakyamuni should not be disturbed in his last hours, Ananda would not permit Subhadra to approach. But Subhadra realized that this was his one and only opportunity to hear the Buddha preach and refused to leave, regardless of how often Ananda urged him to do so.

Shakyamuni heard the talk between the two and called Ananda to his bedside, saying, "Ananda, you must not turn away a person who has come seeking the Law. Bring him here to me."

Subhadra greeted Shakyamuni most respectfully and

asked, "Gautama, all the famous men of religion say that they have attained enlightenment. Is there any truth in what they say?"

Shakyamuni did not answer the question directly but said to Subhadra, "You need not worry about this. The only path that can lead you to true enlightenment is the Eightfold Path of right view, right thinking, right speech, right action, right living, right endeavor, right memory, and right meditation."

As might be expected of one who had spent many years seeking the truth, Subhadra—who is said to have been one hundred twenty years old at that time—immediately understood Shakyamuni's teaching and took refuge in the Three Treasures. Subhadra is remembered as the last person converted to Buddhism by Shakyamuni himself.

Near midnight Shakyamuni called his disciples to his side and said to them, "Monks! If you should have any doubt or illusion about the Buddha, the Law, the Sangha, or the practice of my teaching, ask me while I yet live. After my death it will be too late to regret that you did not do so."

The monks, however, had no questions to ask of Shakyamuni. Their hearts must have been too filled with sorrow at the thought of Shakyamuni's approaching death. Even had they been able to express their thoughts, one can imagine that in their grief their voices would have failed them.

Shakyamuni addressed his disciples two or three times, saying, "Have you anything to ask me?" But they all remained silent. At last Ananda spoke: "World-honored One! It is a rare thing indeed, but there seems to be none among us who has any doubt or illusion."

Hearing Ananda's words, Shakyamuni nodded in

satisfaction and then said to his disciples, "Monks! I will leave words to all of you. All phenomena are always changing. Endeavor to practice my teachings diligently."

Then at midnight Shakyamuni, the greatest sage in history, expired quietly. Although not all Buddhists and scholars are in agreement and there is of course no way of ascertaining the exact date now, February 15 is the date Chinese and Japanese Buddhists observe as the anniversary of the great decease, which occurred around 480 B.C.

The funeral observances and the cremation of Shakyamuni's remains were the same as those then accorded to great kings. The Buddha's relics were taken back to the country of the Shakyas and placed in an urn that remained there nearly twenty-four hundred years, until its discovery in 1898.

During the rainy season following the Buddha's death (though some accounts say it was in the year after his death), five hundred leading disciples, under the guidance of Maha-Kashyapa, gathered for the First Council. At that council the disciples compiled the sutras, containing the Buddha's sermons and the precepts for believers. Because of the faith and devotion of those disciples, the Buddha's teaching has been handed down to us just as he preached it some twenty-five centuries ago and Buddhism remains as vital and practical a religion as it was when its founder was engaged in his great teaching ministry.

Glossary

Where the transliteration of Sanskrit words used in the text differs from the orthodox form, the latter is given in parentheses with full diacritical markings.

Agama (Āgama) sutras   One of the oldest extant Buddhist scriptures, existing in two somewhat different forms: the Pali canon and the Chinese canon.

Ajatashatru (Ajātaśatru)   King of Magadha and son of King Bimbisara.

Ajnata-Kaundinya (Ājñāta-Kauṇḍinya)   One of the five ascetics, the first disciples of Shakyamuni.

Amrapali (Āmrapālī)   A courtesan and follower of Shakyamuni.

Ananda (Ānanda)   A cousin of Shakyamuni and one of the Buddha's ten great disciples. He was famous for his memory and is supposed to have memorized all the Buddha's sermons.

Anathapindada (Anāthapiṇḍada)   "One who gives to the needy," a name given to Sudatta.

Aniruddha   A cousin of Shakyamuni and one of the Buddha's ten great disciples.

Arada-Kalama (Ārāḍa-Kālāma)   A hermit-sage under whom Shakyamuni studied.

arhat   Literally, "man of worth, honorable one." (1) One who is free from all cravings and thus from rebirth. (2) One of the titles of the Buddha.

Ashvajit (Aśvajit)   One of the five ascetics, the first disciples of Shakyamuni.

Asita   The seer who prophesied that if Shakyamuni remained at home he would become a great wheel-rolling king and that if he left home he would become a buddha.

Bamboo Grove (Veṇuvana) Monastery   The first monastery of the Buddhist order, built by King Bimbisara.

Bhadra   A follower of Shakyamuni and the wife of Maha-Kashyapa.

Bhadrika   One of the five ascetics, the first disciples of Shakyamuni.

Bhagavat   World-honored One, an epithet of a buddha.

bhikshu (*bhikṣu*)   Literally, "beggar"; a Buddhist monk.

bhikshuni (*bhikṣuṇī*)   A Buddhist nun.

Bimbisara (Bimbisāra)   King of Magadha and a follower of Shakyamuni.

Bodh Gaya (Buddhagayā)   The place where Shakyamuni Buddha attained enlightenment, near present-day Gaya.

bodhi   Wisdom, enlightenment, buddhahood. The wisdom of Shakyamuni Buddha's enlightenment.

bodhisattva   *Bodhi,* buddhahood; *sattva,* living being. (1) A being in the final stage prior to attaining buddhahood. (2) One who devotes himself to attaining enlightenment not only for himself but also for all sentient beings.

Brahma (Brahmā)   One of the three major deities of Hinduism, adopted as one of the eminent protective deities of Buddhism.

Brahman (*brāhmaṇa*)   A member of the priestly caste, the highest of the four major castes of India.

buddha   A title meaning "one who is enlightened," or "enlightened one."

Chandaka   A servant of Prince Siddhartha (Shakyamuni). He led the horse the prince was riding on the night of his renunciation of the world.

Chunda (Cunda)   A follower of Shakyamuni. He prepared the last meal that the Buddha ate before his death.

Dashabala-Kashyapa (Daśabala-Kāśyapa) A disciple of Sha-kyamuni, he was famous for his supernatural powers.

Deer Park (Mṛgadāva) The park near Varanasi where shortly after his enlightenment Shakyamuni preached his first sermon to five fellow ascetics.

Devadaha The capital city of the Koliya tribe.

Devadatta A cousin of Shakyamuni. He was at first a follower of the Buddha but later left him and attempted to kill him.

dhuta (*dhūta*) An ascetic practice or precept. There are twelve *dhutas,* or mendicant's duties: (1) living in a forest, (2) taking whatever seat might be offered, (3) living on alms, (4) using only one seat for both meditation and eating, (5) wearing coarse garments, (6) not eating at unregulated times, (7) wearing clothes made of discarded rags, (8) having only three robes, (9) living in or near a cemetery, (10) living under a tree, (11) living in the open air, and (12) sleeping in a seated posture.

Eightfold Path Right view, right thinking, right speech, right action, right living, right endeavor, right memory, right meditation.

Evil One *See* Mara.

First Council The first assembly of Buddhist monks, which gathered some three months after the Buddha's death to compile the Buddhist sutras.

five ascetics The five men (Ajnata-Kaundinya, Ashvajit, Bhadrika, Mahanama, and Vashpa) who practiced asceticism with Shakyamuni but left him when he abandoned such practices. After Shakyamuni attained buddhahood his first sermon was preached at Deer Park to these men, who became his first disciples.

Flower Garland (Avataṃsaka) Sutra A lengthy sutra that sets forth the practices of a bodhisattva, as well as other basic Buddhist teachings.

Four Noble Truths (1) All existence entails suffering (the Truth of Suffering). (2) Suffering is caused by ignorance, which gives rise to craving and illusion (the Truth of Cause). (3) There is an end to suffering, and this state of no suffering is called nirvana (the Truth of Extinction). (4)

Nirvana is attained through the practice of the Eightfold Path (the Truth of the Path). This is one of the fundamental doctrines of all forms of Buddhism and was the subject of the first sermon of the Buddha.

Gautama   The surname of the Shakya clan into which Shakyamuni was born. Another name for Shakyamuni.

Gaya-Kashyapa   *See* Kashyapa brothers.

Great Forest (Mahāvana) Monastery   A monastery on the outskirts of Vaishali that Shakyamuni often visited.

Indra   The Hindu deity controlling thunder, lightning, wind, and rain, adopted as one of the eminent protective deities of Buddhism.

Jeta   Crown prince of Kaushala and owner of the land on which the Jetavana Monastery was built.

Jetavana Monastery   The monastery for Shakyamuni and his followers built at Shravasti by Sudatta and Prince Jeta.

Jivaka (Jīvaka)   The physician to King Bimbisara who became a follower of Shakyamuni and also treated the Buddha and his disciples.

Kanthaka (Kaṇṭhaka)   Prince Siddhartha's (Shakyamuni's) horse.

Kapilavastu   The capital of the Shakya kingdom.

karma (*karman*)   The results of actions, which produce effects that may be either good or bad.

Kashyapa (Kāśyapa) brothers   Three brothers, all ascetics, from a Brahman family. The eldest brother, Uruvilva (Uruvilvā), had five hundred disciples; the second brother, Nadi (Nadī), had three hundred disciples; and the youngest brother, Gaya (Gayā), had two hundred disciples. Together with their disciples, the three brothers became followers of Shakyamuni.

Kaushala (Kauśalā)   The most powerful of the sixteen major kingdoms of India in Shakyamuni's time.

Koliya   The country of the Koliya tribe.

Kulika   A wealthy merchant of Varanasi who joined his son, Yashas, in becoming a follower of Shakyamuni.

Kushinagara (Kuśinagara)   The village where Shakyamuni died and the capital of the kingdom of Malla.

Lotus Sutra   The popular name of the Sutra of the Lotus Flower of the Wonderful Law, or Saddharma-puṇḍarīka-sūtra, which consists of a series of sermons delivered by Shakyamuni toward the end of his forty-five-year teaching ministry. One of the most important documents of Mahayana Buddhism, the Lotus Sutra teaches: that all sentient beings can attain Perfect Enlightenment—that is, bud-dhahood—and nothing less than this is the appropriate final goal of believers; that the Buddha is eternal, having existed from the infinite past and appearing in many forms to guide and succor beings through the teaching of the Wonderful Law; and that the noblest form of Buddhist practice is the way of the bodhisattva.

Lumbini (Lumbinī) Garden   The birthplace of Shakyamuni.

Magadha   One of the sixteen major kingdoms of India in Shakyamuni's time.

Maha-Kashyapa (Mahā-Kāśyapa)   One of the ten great dis-ciples of Shakyamuni.

Mahanama (Mahānāma)   One of the five ascetics, the first disciples of Shakyamuni.

Mahaprajapati (Mahāprajāpatī)   The younger sister of Maya, who married King Shuddhodana after Maya's death and raised Shakyamuni. The mother of Nanda, she was the first *bhikshuni* in Buddhism.

Mahayana (Mahāyāna)   Literally, "Great Vehicle." The northern of the two main branches of Buddhism. The southern branch, Theravāda (meaning "Teaching of the Elders" in Pali), which is also known by the Sanskrit name Hīnayāna (literally, "Lesser Vehicle"), spread from India to Sri Lanka, Burma, Thailand, and Cambodia. The Maha-yana branch of Buddhism spread from India to Central Asia, Tibet, Mongolia, China, Korea, and Japan. The Theravada school is based on the Pali canon, while the Mahayana scriptures are recorded in Sanskrit, Tibetan, and Chinese.

Malla   One of the sixteen major kingdoms of India in Sha-kyamuni's time.

Mallika (Mallikā)   The consort of King Prasenajit and a fol-lower of Shakyamuni.

Mara (Māra)   The Evil One (literally, "murderer"), so called because he takes away the wisdom life of all living beings.

Maudgalyayana (Maudgalyāyana)   One of the ten great disciples of Shakyamuni.

Maya (Māyā)   The mother of Shakyamuni, believed to be a princess of the royal house of Koliya. She is also called Mahamaya.

Middle Path   One of the most basic teachings of Buddhism, this is the doctrine of the Middle Path between two extremes, such as self-indulgence and self-mortification.

Mrigara (Mṛgāra)   A wealthy man of Shravasti and a follower of Shakyamuni.

Mrigara-matri (Mṛgāra-mātṛ)   The wife of Mrigara, she donated the land for the edifice known as the Mansion of Mrigara-matri.

Mrigara-matri (Mṛgāra-mātṛ) Hall   A structure near the Jetavana Monastery.

Nadi-Kashyapa   *See* Kashyapa brothers.

Nanda   The younger half brother of Shakyamuni and one of the ten great disciples of the Buddha.

nirvana (*nirvāṇa*)   Literally, "extinction." (1) The state of enlightenment attained by the Buddha. (2) The highest state of enlightenment. (3) Emancipation from all forms of existence.

Pataliputra (Pāṭaliputra)   Present-day Patna, in the state of Bihar.

Pava (Pāvā)   The village where Shakyamuni ate the meal that led to his final illness.

Perfect Wisdom (Prajñāpāramitā) sutras   A group of sutras setting forth the doctrine of the Void (*śūnyatā*).

Piprahwa   The Indian village southeast of Lumbini, thought to be Kapilavastu, near which an urn containing the relics of Shakyamuni was excavated from an ancient tomb in 1898.

Prasenajit   The king of Kaushala who together with his wife and son became a follower of Shakyamuni.

Rahula (Rāhula)   The son of the Buddha, born before Shakyamuni's renunciation of the world. He is one of the ten great disciples of Shakyamuni.

Rajagriha (Rājagṛha)   Present-day Rajgir, in the state of Bihar; the capital of the ancient kingdom of Magadha.

Sangha (saṃgha)   The monastic community of Buddhist monks or nuns; more generally, the community of Buddhist believers. Or more generally the whole of Mankind. Or hereafter,

Sanjaya (Sañjaya)   One of the six non-Buddhist teachers.

Shakya (Śākya)   The tribe to which Shakyamuni belonged.

Shakyamuni (Śākyamuni)   Literally, "Sage of the Shakyas." The usual Mahayana Buddhist appellation of the historical Buddha.

shala (śala) grove   The stand of twin-trunked shala (or possibly teak) trees near Kushinagara where Shakyamuni died.

Shariputra (Śāriputra)   The foremost of the ten great disciples of Shakyamuni.

Shravasti (Śrāvastī)   The capital of the kingdom of Kaushala.

Shuddhodana (Śuddhodana)   King of the Shakyas and father of Shakyamuni, whose follower he became.

Siddhartha (Siddhārtha)   Literally, "he who has accomplished his aim." The personal name of the historical Buddha before his renunciation of the world.

Subhadra   A man who became Shakyamuni's disciple shortly before the latter's death.

Sudatta   A wealthy merchant of Shravasti and a follower of Shakyamuni. He purchased the land on which the Jetavana Monastery was built.

Sujata (Sujātā)   The village girl who gave Shakyamuni a bowl of rice gruel before his attainment of enlightenment.

Sutra of the Great Decease (Mahā-parinirvāṇa-sūtra)   The sutra in which are recorded the final sermon, the death, and the funeral of Shakyamuni.

Svastika   Literally, "well-being" or "good fortune." The youth who gave Shakyamuni a basket of sweet grass on which the Buddha sat while attaining enlightenment.

Tathagata (Tathāgata)   Literally, "one who has thus gone," that is, one who has reached the truth and come to declare it; the highest epithet of a buddha.

Theravada   See Mahayana.

Three Treasures   The Buddha; the Law, or Teaching, of the Buddha; and the Sangha, or community of believers.

Udayin (Udāyin)   A childhood friend of Shakyamuni who became one of his disciples.

Udraka-Ramaputra (Udraka-Rāmaputra)   A hermit-sage under whom Shakyamuni studied.

Upali (Upāli)   One of the ten great disciples of the Buddha. A former slave, he became a monk and was very strict in his observance of the precepts.

upasaka (upāsaka)   A male lay believer of Buddhism.

upasika (upāsikā)   A female lay believer of Buddhism.

Uruvilva-Kashyapa   *See* Kashyapa brothers.

Vaishali (Vaiśālī)   The chief city of the Vriji tribes.

Varanasi (Vārāṇasī)   A city on the Ganges also known as Benares; the capital of the ancient kingdom of Kashi.

varshika (vārṣika)   A retreat or spiritual training during the rainy season.

Vashpa (Vāṣpa)   One of the five ascetics, the first disciples of Shakyamuni.

Vaidehi (Vaidehī)   The wife of King Bimbisara and the mother of King Ajatashatru.

Vriji (Vṛji)   A major tribal confederation, one of the sixteen major kingdoms of India in Shakyamuni's time.

Vulture Peak (Gṛdhrakūṭa)   A mountain near present-day Rajgir, Bihar; its name is said to derive from the fact that its peak is shaped like a vulture and also that many vultures are supposed to have lived on the mountain.

wheel-rolling king *(cakravarti-rāja)*   (1) In Indian mythology, the ideal ruler. (2) In Buddhist terms there are four such kings, each with a precious wheel of gold, silver, copper, or iron. The kings reign over the four great regions, north, south, east, and west. The king of the gold wheel rules the entire world; the king of the silver wheel the east, west, and south regions; the king of the copper wheel the east and south; the king of the iron wheel the south alone.

World-honored One   *See Bhagavat.*

Yashas (Yaśas)   An early convert of Shakyamuni.

Yashodhara (Yaśodharā)   The wife of Shakyamuni before he renounced the world and the mother of Rahula; she later became a *bhikshuni*.